James,

God getting
this year.
of you at waterrock and
CM next year. Have a
good summer.

God bless,
Justin

SWEAR
TO GOD

SWEAR TO GOD

The Promise and Power of the Sacraments

SCOTT HAHN

DOUBLEDAY

New York • London • Toronto • Sydney • Auckland

PUBLISHED BY DOUBLEDAY
a division of Random House, Inc.

DOUBLEDAY and the portrayal of an anchor with a dolphin
are registered trademarks of Random House, Inc.

Library of Congress Cataloging-in-Publication Data
Hahn, Scott.
Swear to God : the promise and power of the Sacraments /
Scott Hahn.— 1st ed.
p. cm.
Includes bibliographical references.
1. Sacraments—Catholic church. I. Title.
BX2200H24   2003
234'.16—dc22   2003070006

ISBN 0-385-50931-6

June 2004

5   7   9   10   8   6

To Jeremiah

CONTENTS

CHAPTER 1

✺✺✺

"A BORE,"
I SWORE

I WAS THE kind of first-year graduate student who believed in his own resume. I had arrived, on scholarship, at a prestigious evangelical seminary after a stellar undergraduate career—and in the first semester of my master's program, I'd scored straight As.

It was second semester now, and I walked the scenic hundred acres of Gordon-Conwell Theological Seminary as if they were my inheritance. Beside me walked my bright and beautiful bride, who was also a graduate student. Kimberly and I were newlyweds, and when I held forth on any subject, her face radiated love, intelligent interest, and, usually, perfect agreement. Her loveliness and her love for me seemed a visible sign of God's blessing upon my life—and a seal on my high self-estimation.

No one was as sure of the law of gravity as I was sure of the soundness of my judgments.

One afternoon, Kimberly and I were leaving class when we saw a friend of ours in the building's vestibule. George was a good fellow. He was a highly motivated student, like me. And he considered himself a staunch Calvinist, though I rated myself even stauncher. George was also a voracious reader, like me. So whenever I saw him with new books, I'd ask him for titles. That afternoon, he was carrying books. "So, George, what are you reading," I asked, "anything good?"

His eyes lit up. "Yes, Scott!" And he shook a book out from the middle of the pile. "Calvin on the sacraments."

I took the book and looked at its drab cover: *Calvin's Doctrine of the Word and Sacraments,* by Ronald S. Wallace. As surely as George's eyes lit up, mine must have dimmed. I handed it back to him and blurted out the first thing that came to my mind: "Frankly, George, sacraments bore me."

I was merely speaking honestly. Though I didn't care to admit it, I often found myself distracted in church, my mind wandering, when the time came to administer baptism or the Lord's Supper. Ritual was not the thing that got me up early and kept me up late. I was hungry for dynamic biblical teaching and preaching; and sacraments suggested, to my mind at least, the exact opposite: a mechanical way of approaching religion—ritualistic, ceremonial, bordering on superstitious.

In any event, the sacraments were peripheral to most Protestant discussions of salvation and justification, the matters that really interested me.

Sacraments—well, frankly, they bored me, and I said so.

Bored Again

I hadn't meant to say anything rude or scandalous. But I could see right away that I had. No one responded. Kimberly just arched an eyebrow in silent shock. George took his book back with a polite smile and a shrug and said he had to be going.

Kimberly and I continued out the door and on to dinner. I asked her why my simple statement had been such an immediate conversation-stopper.

She looked at me with a pained smile and repeated what I had said: "Sacraments . . . bore me." After a pause, she added, "Scott, I don't think it's *safe* to say that."

It helped that she was a pastor's daughter. She went on to explain that, no matter how I felt about the sacraments, it was clear from the Scriptures that Jesus Christ had established both baptism and the Lord's Supper. She reminded me that, in the previous semester, one of my favorite professors, M. G. Kline, an Old Testament scholar, had convinced us to see the sacraments as "covenant oaths" that sealed and renewed our personal relationship with Jesus Christ. To dismiss these oaths was to flirt with ingratitude and maybe even blasphemy.

Kimberly brought my lesson to a close with a smile and a pun. "Don't be surprised, Scott," she said, "when you go before the Lord, if you discover that sacraments truly 'bore' you—all the way to heaven!"

I wasn't so sure. But still, I'd begun to trust her intuitions. After finding a copy of the book that George was reading, I discovered why he was so excited. Over the following months, I found myself learning more about the sacraments in dynamic terms. I started to see their drama, passion, grandeur, splendor, promise, and power.

I soon ranked the Wallace book among my favorites. A few years later, when I was a Protestant minister teaching in a Protestant seminary, I even used it as a course textbook.

Signs, Signs, Everywhere a Sign

My education in the sacraments was only beginning. As a Protestant, I recognized only two of the seven sacraments observed by the Catholic Church: baptism and the Lord's Supper, and I knew them only in a limited way, as Calvinist doctrine stops far short of the "realism" that marks the Catholic tradition of the sacraments.

Still, as I read the Bible, I began to glimpse something more. Since Kimberly had shaken me out of my complacency, I was struck by certain details I had always glossed over. Now I noticed that God had a particular and characteristic way of dealing with His people down through the ages. He made *covenants* with them, and He always sealed those covenants not with an abstract lecture on the nature of salvation, obligation, and law but with an outward sign, a *physical* sign. When God made His covenant with Noah, He set a rainbow in the sky as a "sign of the covenant" (Gen 9:12). When God made His covenant with Abraham,

5

He instructed the patriarch to have "every male among you . . . circumcised" (Gen 17:10). When God made His covenant with Moses, Moses extended it to the people by sprinkling them with the blood of sacrificial animals: "Behold the blood of the covenant which the Lord has made with you" (Ex 24:8).

These words and signs in the Old Testament would come to fulfillment in the New Testament. Jesus would speak of His saving work as a "new covenant in My blood" (Lk 22:20), and He would announce this at the moment He established the sacrament of the Eucharist, or the "Lord's Supper," as we Presbyterians called it.

Moreover, Jesus spoke of the sacraments as essential to salvation. Of baptism, He said, "unless one is born of water and the Spirit, he cannot enter the kingdom of God" (Jn 3:5). Of the Eucharist, He said, "unless you eat of the flesh of the Son of man and drink His blood, you have no life in you" (Jn 6:53).

The sacraments, then, were anything but boring. They were actions with ultimate consequences. They were matters of life and death, heaven or hell. God Himself spoke of them only in the most dramatic of terms. Jesus' apostles remained faithful to His example, and they too put matters starkly. St. Paul warned that Christians who lacked proper reverence for the sacraments brought divine judgment upon themselves and were justly punished with illnesses and even death (see 1 Cor 11:29–30). Kimberly had good reason, then, to wonder about the safety of someone who belittled the sacraments, especially when that someone was an aspiring theologian—and her husband.

Get Real

Because of a providential encounter with a fellow student, I learned to read the Scriptures in a new way, a sacramental way. And I could not help but be changed by the sacramental story I began to piece together. The Bible, in both the Old and New Testaments, seemed to speak of God's sacraments with a powerful realism. These actions were symbolic, but they were more than *just* symbols. They were memorials, but they were not *just* reminders. They were rites of passage, but they were more than *just* rituals. The sacraments were divine actions on the order of the creation of the universe. They marked the moments in history—world history, salvation history, and personal history—when God was making a new start with His people.

This idea pervaded the Scriptures. And Kimberly and George seemed to hold it instinctively; that's what made them wince when I professed my boredom with sacraments. Yet, as I studied the matter, I was troubled that I could not find support for such "sacramental realism" in the works of my Protestant forebears or their most ardent contemporary followers.

It should have been easy, then, for me to dismiss my "discovery" as a fantasy, a false reading. But I soon began to find that sacramental realism expressed in other, unexpected places. I found it everywhere, for example, in the writings of the earliest Christian writers, the fathers of the Church. The founder of my particular kind of Protestantism, John Calvin, had placed a high value on the testimony of the fathers. So I felt comfortable approaching them for light on the Scriptures. I began to notice, however, that the early-Christian view of the sacraments was anything but Calvinist—yet it seemed to be more compatible with the Bible.

My reading in the fathers eventually led me out of the ancient world, as I found the biblical teaching on the sacraments reflected in the place I least expected: the teaching and practice of the Roman Catholic Church.

Since being "born again" as a teenager, I had been a devoted son of the Protestant Reformation. Indeed, I longed for the day when I would preach the Gospel from a pulpit in a Presbyterian church. I believed the doctrines of Calvin and Luther—and their rejection of Catholicism—to be a recovery of true biblical principles. Everything I knew about Catholic doctrine I had learned second- or third-hand, from the Catholic Church's opponents.

Worshipping with Heart

But I was about to learn the truth, a truth that many millions of holy and humble souls had learned long before me. It was a truth that even some Protestant theologians had reluctantly come to admit. The nineteenth-century Lutheran scholar Julius Wellhausen said that "Protestant worship is at bottom Catholic worship . . . with the heart taken out of it." That heart, said the Catholic theologian Karl Adam, is "the Catholic's experience of reality in the great Mystery, his assurance that in it the grace of Christ really and truly enters our world of space and time and touches his soul."

Karl Adam summed up the principle as "the idea of real divine grace sacramentally conveyed"—in baptism, in the Mass, in confession, in confirmation, in marriage, in the ordination of priests, and in the anointing of the sick. He called it, succinctly, "the Catholic sacramental idea." He could just as accurately have called it "the biblical sacramental idea."

In a matter of a few years, I would admit that the two were identical, and I would be received into the Catholic Church. In a few more years, my wife, Kimberly, would follow.

We found in the sacraments what Catholics take in with mother's milk. After much searching, we found the biblical and Catholic "sacramental idea" that ordinary parishioners learn from earliest infancy, as they see the sights, hear the sounds, taste the flavors, feel the texture, and smell the aromas of the seven sacraments. God makes His covenant with Catholic Christians—as He did with Noah, Abraham, Moses, and David—using material signs: water and oil, bread and wine, a touch of the hands upon the shoulders, an audible word of blessing.

Still, I wouldn't be surprised, today, to learn that more than a few Catholics feel what I felt, so long ago, as a Calvinist. They find sacraments boring, but only because they haven't learned (or perhaps they've forgotten) the splendor and the drama of Christ's saving doctrine. They've stopped noticing how the sacraments have borne them up till now and promise to bear them to heaven.

On a winter afternoon, on the lovely grounds of that New England seminary, Kimberly and George had given me a first lesson, a basic lesson, in the meaning of the sacraments. I had prided myself as a prodigy in theology. God showed me that I was still a beginner and that I had much learning and growing to do.

There were many more lessons to come, and those are the lessons that fill the rest of these pages. Some I learned from books. Some I learned through experience, conversation, and tears.

In the Catholic Church, I learned what sacraments really are and how Christ established them. I learned that at the heart of every biblical covenant there is a solemn and sacramental oath. I learned that these oaths contained real power to change lives and change history. And I learned that the sacraments still pack that power today.

CHAPTER 2

❦❦❦

SIGNS AND
MYSTERIES

M Y NEWFOUND INTEREST in the sacraments required constant feeding with books. I was
building up, quite laboriously, to the doctrine
that my Catholic contemporaries had learned in simple
formulas in their religion classes. The *Baltimore Catechism*
summed it up for American parishes a generation ago: "A
sacrament is an outward sign instituted by Christ to give
grace. . . . The sacraments receive their power to give
grace from God, through the merits of Jesus Christ."

There's a lot packed into those few words, but by
themselves they're not enough to bear a Calvinist, or even
a Catholic, out of his boredom with sacramental rituals.
Indeed, those old definitions are themselves most useful as
signs. They point us to the mystical heights and doctrinal
depths of sacramental theology, but they don't take us
there. They're meant to be a beginning, but they're a necessary beginning. We need to read those signs carefully so
that we arrive safely at our destination, and by the most

direct route. So, in this chapter, we'll review the Church's basic teaching on the sacraments.

Power Lines

The *Catechism of the Catholic Church* had not yet been written when I first began to research the sacraments. It is an enormous advantage to us as we approach the sacraments today.

The traditional definition is very good, as far as it goes. But it doesn't really explain fully what sacraments are. The *Baltimore Catechism* explained where sacraments come from: They are instituted by Christ. It explained what they do: They give grace, which is a share in God's life. But it did not explain what sacraments are other than that they are "outward signs"—a somewhat circular definition.

The *Catechism of the Catholic Church* reaches into the Scriptures to assemble a more engaging definition: "Sacraments are 'powers that come forth' from the Body of Christ, which is ever-living and life-giving. They are actions of the Holy Spirit at work in His Body, the Church. They are 'the masterworks of God' in the new and everlasting covenant" (n. 1116).

In just a few words, this definition evokes some of the memorable moments of Jesus' ministry: the moments when He healed people. In the press of a crowd, Jesus said, "Someone touched Me; for I perceive that power has gone forth from me" (Lk 8:46), and immediately the anonymous woman was cured of her chronic hemorrhage. "And all the crowd sought to touch Him, for power came forth from Him and healed them all" (Lk 6:19).

This, it seems, is the essence of Jesus' ministry. "God so loved the world" that He "became flesh and dwelt among us" (Jn 3:16, 1:14). He had a human body, so that we could see Him and touch Him; and through His touch, He brought healing to "all the crowd." His physical cures win our attention, but these are not His most important works. He Himself subordinated these miracles to the spiritual miracle of salvation from sins. On one occasion, He made the matter clear: "Which is easier, to say to the paralytic, 'Your sins are forgiven,' or to say, 'Rise, take up your pallet and walk'?" (Mk 2:9). The answer is supposed to be obvious to us.

Jesus came to bring *salvation,* a word that, in the ancient languages, is synonymous with health and safety. His physical cures were "outward signs" of a deeper and more lasting spiritual healing. Presumably, all of the people He cured during His ministry eventually died. Presumably, then, their physical cure was of secondary importance, subordinate to an enduring healing, a spiritual healing, that would survive even the death of the body.

Though His healings were primarily spiritual, Jesus still worked them by physical means—by anointing a man with mud and spittle (Jn 9:6–7), by His spoken words (Mk 10:52), or merely by making eye contact (Lk 22:61).

Why would God manifest His power by such ordinary, earthy means? He did not need to become a man in order to work miracles. God can and He does work wonders from heaven. It was not for His sake that He took flesh, but for ours. He made us, and so He knows that we human beings learn through sensible signs, sensory data. You know the old saying: Seeing is believing. It is possible, of course, to believe without seeing, but God is willing to accommodate our human condition to a remarkable degree (see Jn 20:24–29).

What's more, He intended His work not just for His small number of contacts in an obscure land, in the brief time of His ministry. He wanted everyone to experience His presence and His healing touch. He established the Church on earth so that He could extend His incarnation through time and space. Thus He commanded His priests to celebrate the sacraments with Him—through all time—on earth. Baptize all nations, He told the apostles (see Mt 28:19). And of the Eucharist He said, "Do this in remembrance of Me" (1 Cor 11:24). The rest of the New Testament testifies that the apostles did as He had commanded. When they established the Church in a new place, they baptized, they gathered for the Eucharist, they ordained priests, they anointed the sick.

By the power of the Holy Spirit, the Church has continued to do the works of God incarnate. The Church is His living body (1 Cor 12:12–27, Col 1:24, Rom 12:5) and power comes forth from it, from the day of Pentecost "to the close of the age" (Mt 28:20).

The sacraments have an impressive historical pedigree, but they do not depend upon it. For they are the actions not merely of priests who come and go, but of Jesus Christ Who lives. We do not speak of Him in the past tense, as if He were a figure we read about in books of ancient history. We say "Jesus *is* risen," and we meet Him alive in the sacraments. We celebrate the sacraments—we "do this"— because *this* is what He wants us to do. Jesus Himself established the sacraments as the ordinary means of extending salvation to each and every person.

The Science of Signs

Why did Jesus choose to communicate His salvation through signs? Because that is the way humans express themselves.

A sign is something used to represent something else. All words are signs, but words are not the only signs. A flag, for example, represents a country. Our respect for the flag does not arise from the value of the cloth. The honor we show the flag symbolizes our respect for the country. When protesters want to show their disrespect for a country, they sometimes will deface or destroy its flag.

A sign is a visible symbol of something that's invisible at the moment. We can see a flag, but we cannot see the entire country, much less the ideals embodied by the nation's government. The flag is the symbol of the country, its people, and its principles.

A sign reveals something about the object it represents. A United States flag shows, by its fifty stars, that there are fifty states in the union; the red stripes memorialize those who died in serving their country; the white stripes stand for purity; and blue symbolizes heaven.

Yet a sign also conceals much about the object it represents. For signs and things remain distinct. A flag is not a country; and even though we might spend years studying the flag, the nation itself will elude definition. The nation, in a sense, is a mysterious reality—a mystery.

A sacrament is like other signs, but also unlike them.

Like other signs, a sacrament signifies invisible realities, but its symbolic value is infinitely richer. Consider the baptism of a baby. The infant is three times washed in water while a priest or deacon pronounces a blessing. The washing represents the forgiveness of sins. The triple immersion in water, moreover, symbolizes Christ's burial for three days; in baptism, all Christians participate in Christ's saving death (see Rom 6:3). Yet the emergence from water also signifies the baby's resurrection with Christ—a new birth to divine life (see Tit 3:5).

And there is still more. Baptism evokes many scenes from the Bible, not least the baptism of Jesus (Mk 1:9–11). The blessing of the water signifies the Spirit moving over the waters at the moment of creation (Gen 1:2). The washing is a sign of the cleansing waters of the great flood (Gen 7–9); the passing of Israel through the Red Sea (Ex 14:21–22); the river flowing through the heavenly Jerusalem (Rev 22:1); and much more.

Sacramental signs represent many realities all at once—or at least a many-faceted divine reality.

Into the Mysteries

But there is a more important way in which sacraments differ from other signs, and we hinted at it in the last chapter, when we spoke of the Church's sacramental realism. For sacraments are symbols, but they are not merely symbols. They are symbols that genuinely convey the reality they signify.

All other signs remain distinct from the things they signify. Only sacraments bring about what they signify. Ordinary signs convey an idea about something. Sacramental signs convey the sacred reality itself.

There can be no more perfect communication than this. Only God could express Himself in this way.

To describe the sacraments as "mysteries" seems like stating the obvious, almost a redundancy. Indeed, for the early Christians, the two words, "sacrament" and "mystery," were synonyms. If there is a shade of difference, it is this: The word "sacrament" emphasizes the visible sign; the word "mystery" emphasizes the invisible reality (see CCC, n. 1075). The word "mystery" continues to be the preferred term in the Christian churches of the East.

In preaching on the sacraments in the year 445, Pope Leo the Great said, "What was visible in our Savior has passed over into His mysteries."

Social Graces

The sacraments, then, could only be divine actions, works of Christ. He has, however, entrusted the sacraments to the Church. He made His priests to be "stewards of the mysteries of God" (1 Cor 4:1).

Even so, when a priest celebrates the sacraments, his work is secondary to that of Jesus Christ. Thus, the sacraments do not depend upon the strength, the skill, the intelligence, the eloquence, or even the holiness of the individual priest. For it is Christ who acts—though through His unworthy minister—in every sacrament. St. Augustine put it in a memorable way: "When Peter baptizes, it is Christ Who baptizes. . . . When Judas baptizes, it is Christ Who baptizes." Elsewhere he said it still more bluntly: "Those whom a drunkard baptized, those whom a murderer baptized, those whom an adulterer baptized, if it was the baptism of Christ, were baptized by Christ."

Every sacrament produces its effects by the power of Christ alone, and not at all by our own labors or the labors of our priest. The Latin theological term for this is *ex opere operato*—literally, "by the very fact of the action's being performed"—which denotes its intrinsic power and efficacy (see CCC, n. 1128).

The effect of the sacraments, however, depends upon

how well we are disposed to receive them. Christ always gives grace in the sacraments; but we must have the right motives and conditions for receiving that grace.

These are very important principles to keep in mind. There was a time, before I was a Catholic, when I looked upon sacraments as mechanical or magical actions. I believed Catholics were misguided in thinking that mere rituals could manipulate God. But I was wrong about all of this. For it was Christ Who established the sacraments, and He did so for our sake. We do not force His hand when we celebrate the rites. We cannot manipulate God. Nor can we grab hold of divine life if we are not disposed to live it.

God established the sacraments because He knows our needs. He loves like a Father, and He leads us like a master teacher. Why else would He command us to "do this" and to baptize—to go through the motions of a ritual?

I, too, am a father and a teacher, and sometimes I think I glimpse what God is doing. At home, I teach my younger children to say "please" if they ask for anything, even if they're asking for something I'm certain to give them. ("Please pass the spinach.") I do this for their good, because the exercise builds up good outward habits and inward dispositions. What's more, unless they go through the exercise, they will almost certainly grow up lacking certain virtues—certain social "graces." They will be impolite, and so incapable of many joys of human society. In a similar way, the sacramental rituals strengthen us in the divine grace we need to enjoy the divine society, the communion of saints.

Rituals are important in the natural order, and sacramental rituals work supernatural marvels *ex opere operato*. But the priests who celebrate these sacraments are not magicians. They are fathers, and they are stewards of Christ's mysteries. This is one reason why the Church concerns itself with the "form" and "matter" used in its sacramental rites. The Church exercises good stewardship by ensuring that the rites retain their value as signs, so that they can accurately communicate the doctrine and the reality intended by Jesus Christ. Thus, no priest may change the ritual form or use different matter—for example, by baptizing in wine instead of water, or saying Mass with rice bread instead of wheat, or by improvising his own liturgical text. The sacraments belong to Christ, and they are entrusted to the Church. The Catholic clergy are their ministers and stewards.

God gave us sacraments because He knows we need them, He knows how we learn, He knows how to Father.

It's All Good

The sacraments are built upon the theological principle that creation is good. God made the world, and He saw that what He made was "very good" (Gen 1:31). It isn't just the spiritual side of human life that is good while the material, physical life is evil. That view has always been rejected by the Church as heresy. Christians believe that all creation is good, as God made it.

Sin radically affected all creation, both spiritually and materially, but it did not destroy nature's goodness. Indeed, how did Christ accomplish our redemption? It was precisely by taking upon Himself human nature—not just a spiritual human soul, but also a physical human body. He took on our flesh in the Incarnation and He resurrected that flesh, as well; and that flesh and blood, that very human body, is enthroned in glory in heaven.

Our Savior did not despise living in a virginal womb for nine months, as physical as that was, or nursing at His mother's breast for three years, or growing up as a young child, or growing tired, weeping, and bleeding as a grown man. Why? Because Jesus Christ Who is the Redeemer of the world is also the Creator. So the one Who made matter and spirit redeems matter and spirit; and He uses matter and spirit to redeem us, as well. In His earthly life and in His sacramental mysteries, Jesus Christ, the Creator and Redeemer of the world, uses matter, physical reality, to accomplish our redemption.

The Church is the extension of Christ's incarnation, and that extension takes place through the sacraments. God does extraordinary things through ordinary means. He uses the natural to do the supernatural, the human to accomplish the divine. So the sacraments, in sum, constitute the very heart of the Catholic faith and worship.

Yet, as great as the sacraments are, they are not permanent institutions. They are our participation now in a life we hope one day to know more fully. When Christ comes in glory, all sacraments will cease. Now we know Him through signs, as through a glass darkly (1 Cor 13:12). Then we will see Him as He is (1 Jn 3:2), and we will have no need of signs.

CHAPTER 3

❧❧❧

SACRAMENTS IN
THE SCRIPTURES

IN THE YEARS before I was Catholic, I had many mistaken notions about the sacraments. (How else could they have bored me?) For as long as I could, for example, I clung to the notion that the whole sacramental "system" was a late invention—a compromise struck by the emperor's church in the fourth century, to make pagan converts feel more at home with the Roman Empire's only legal religion. I liked the phrase "sacramental system" because it suggested something institutional, something without heart. And that's how I viewed the matter.

When I spoke about the Catholic Church's sacraments, I would set them as something unnecessarily elaborate, in contrast to the simplicity of the Bible, the unadorned Word of God.

It was, however, the Bible that made me see the error of my ways.

Reads Like Teen Spirit

As I studied for the Protestant ministry—and, even more, after I was ordained a minister—reading the Bible was more than an occupation for me. It was a preoccupation.

I had been "born again" as a teenager, and at fifteen, I asked the Lord to give me a hunger for His Word, to make me burn with excitement for the Bible. I received that gift, full force, one Sunday morning, when I was sitting alone at home. From that night on—I can't explain it—my appetite for the Scriptures was voracious. I began to take my Bible with me everywhere; I read it whenever I could. Just a year before, I had been a troublemaking teenager, sneaking smokes between classes. Now I was sneaking the sacred page.

By the time I entered seminary, I had been poring over the Scriptures for the better part of a decade. I had read the entire Bible many times through, and yet each reading brought new discoveries. The Spirit seemed to hold back certain truths until I was ready for them—and then suddenly dazzle me as if they were the most stunning and obvious things on the page.

That's the way it was with my belated discovery of the sacraments. I have no doubt that my wife was led by the Holy Spirit when she shook me out of my boredom. Ever after, not only did I find sacraments interesting, I found them everywhere in the Bible.

That, too, is Catholic teaching (though I didn't know

it at the time), and it has been since the time of the most ancient fathers.

Rock Festival

In the New Testament, St. Paul himself made the connection, stating that his Israelite ancestors had "passed through the sea, and all were baptized into Moses in the cloud and in the sea, and all ate the same supernatural food and all drank the same supernatural drink. For they drank from the supernatural Rock which followed them, and the Rock was Christ" (1 Cor 10:2–4). In the same letter, he speaks of Christian worship as the "new festival" of "unleavened bread," where Christ is "our paschal lamb" (5:7–8). The new festival had been foreshadowed, then, in the great festival of the Old Testament: the Passover of ancient Israel.

For St. Paul, and for the earliest Christian interpreters of the Bible, the Church's sacraments do not appear on the scene suddenly, as some sort of novelty, or as something incidental to the story. Rather, they bring to light what had long been in shadows; they bring to fulfillment what had been inchoate since the dawn of creation. Indeed, in a sense, they themselves are the fulfillment of God's promises from the beginning.

All seven sacraments are actions of Jesus Christ. In Christ, heaven and earth meet, time and eternity unite most fruitfully. Christ is God incarnate, Word become flesh (Jn 1:14). In Christ, and in His sacraments, there is a marital bond between God and man, between the invisible and the visible. This is what is "new" about the New Testament. It is new, but it is *not* an innovation. It does *not* mark a revolution in the way God deals with humankind. It does not mean the undoing of the sacred history that had passed till then. In fact, it is the culmination, the peak, the very point, of all previous history.

Jesus renewed something; and He took it, as only He could, to its divinely intended completion.

What's the Matter?

As I said in the first chapter of this book, God has a certain characteristic way of dealing with His people. It is not wrapped up in words so much as signs. It is sacramental. This was true from the first moment of creation, and it is just as true today. It is evident throughout the Old Testament, where God's Chosen People spoke of all creation in profoundly sacramental terms:

> *The heavens are telling the glory of God;*
> *and the firmament proclaims His handiwork. . . .*
> *There is no speech, nor are there words;*
> *their voice is not heard;*
> *yet their voice goes out through all the earth. (Ps 19:1–4)*

God tends not to work in abstractions. His word is not mere words; it is creative, living, and active. The *Catechism of the Catholic Church* puts it well: "God speaks to man through the visible creation. The material cosmos is so presented to man's intelligence that he can read there traces of its Creator. Light and darkness, wind and fire, water and earth, the tree and its fruit speak of God and symbolize both His greatness and His nearness" (n. 1147).

God created the physical universe; He made it good; and He did not hesitate to use its most commonplace items to manifest His glory. Sometimes, too, God would even elevate those commonplace items for uncommon purposes, as channels of divine power.

The early Christians saw this clearly. In the year A.D. 383, St. Gregory of Nyssa preached a sermon in which he cited many sacramental uses of nature in the Old Testament: "Moses' rod was a hazel switch—common wood that any hands might cut and carry and use as they please before tossing it into the fire. But God wanted to work miracles through that rod—great miracles, beyond the power of words to express [see Ex 4–14]. . . . Likewise, the mantle of one of the prophets, a simple goatskin, made Elisha famous throughout the whole world [see 2 Kgs 2:8]. . . . A bramble bush showed the presence of God to Moses [see Ex 3:2]. The remains of Elisha raised a dead man to life [see 2 Kgs 13:21]."

St. John of Damascus added: "I do not worship matter; I worship the creator of matter Who became matter for my sake, Who willed to take His abode in matter; who worked out my salvation through matter. Never will I cease honoring the matter which wrought my salvation! . . . God has filled it with His grace and power. Through it my salvation has come to me."

Creation, then, could serve as a natural sacrament. Nature itself was a sign, but God showed it capable of conveying supernatural power as well.

Natural Rites

It was not in nature, however, that St. Paul found the preeminent sacraments of the Old Testament. He looked instead to ancient Israel's ritual worship. Abraham and all of his male descendants had "cut" their covenant with God by the rite of circumcision. The New Testament even identifies the Old Covenant with its sacramental sign when Stephen refers to "the covenant of circumcision" (Acts 7:8).

We learn from St. Paul, however, that the Old Covenant and the old sacrament—great as they were— foreshadowed something still greater: "you were circumcised with a circumcision made without hands, by putting off the body of flesh in the circumcision of Christ; and you were buried with Him in baptism" (Col 2:11-12). The circumcision of infants prefigured the baptism of those who would be "newborn" in Christ. The old rite marked a child's "birth" as a son of Abraham; the new rite marks the still greater birth of a child of God.

We saw earlier, with St. Paul, that the ancient Passover meal served as the renewal of the Old Covenant. Israelites sacrificed the paschal lamb so that their firstborn children would be spared the plague of death. In the New Testament, it was at a Passover meal that Jesus established the New Covenant in His blood (1 Cor 11:25). With the traditional unleavened bread and cups of wine, Jesus offered the first Mass at the Passover seder on the night He was betrayed (see Lk 22:15 and CCC, n. 1340).

In baptism and Eucharist, Christ's action was "new" in the sense of a renewal; but it was not a novelty. It did not abolish the Old Testament, but fulfilled it and renewed it in a transformative way. The same could be said of all the sacraments (see CCC, n. 1150). They had been implicit in all God's dealings with His beloved Israel and with all of mankind. They would be explicit with the revelation of the Church.

How Do You Figure?

We have spoken of certain Old Testament events as "shadows" and "figures." In these, the sacraments of Jesus Christ are foreshadowed, prefigured. The New Testament uses a specific Greek term for the process. It is *tupos,* sometimes rendered in English as "type" (see CCC, n. 1094).

In the Letter to the Hebrews, we find the tabernacle and its rituals described as "types and shadows of heavenly realities" (8:5) and the law as a "shadow of the good things to come" (10:1). St. Peter noted that Noah and his family "were saved through water" and that "this prefigured baptism, which saves you now" (1 Pet 3:20–21). Peter's word translated as "prefigured" is actually the Greek word for *typify,* or "make a type."

The study of such biblical foreshadowings is called "typology" (see CCC, nn. 123–130).

Why do the Scriptures work this way? St. Augustine explained that ordinary human writers use words to signify things; but God uses even created things to signify things. So not only are the *words* of Scripture signs of things that happened in history, but the *very events of sacred history* were fashioned by God as material signs that show us immaterial realities—temporal events that disclose eternal truths. God writes the world the way men write words (see CCC, nn. 116–117).

Thus we can read the Scriptures at once as a kind of divine poetry and as the sacred history of the world. The two are not incompatible. In typology, we discover God's rhyme scheme in history.

Economic Growth

What, then, is the form of the poem? Where do the rhymes occur? How should we approach our study of the Bible's typology? It can be helpful to look at Scripture's narrative as a gradual revelation of divine truth, unfolding in three successive stages:

1. The age of nature, from the creation of the world, through the era of the patriarchs, to the time of Moses

2. The age of law, beginning with the giving of the

law to Moses on Mount Sinai and continuing through the history of ancient Israel

3. The age of grace, begun with the advent of Jesus Christ

These three ages, first sketched out by St. Paul (Rom 5:12–14), culminate, in the end, in glory—in the full revelation of God at the consummation of history.

St. Thomas Aquinas read the Bible this way. He saw all the Scriptures as constituting a single narrative—a single "divine economy." The Bible tells the story of how God prepared the world for Christ, how Christ came to fulfill those preparations, and how Christ will come again in glory to bring His work to completion. Since the sacraments were essential to Christ's saving work, they were very much in the mind of God "in the beginning," and they were an important part of the historical preparation for the Messiah.

St. Thomas saw the role that water played in this cosmic drama. In the age of nature, water was a natural sacrament, "suggested in the first production of things, when the Spirit of God hovered over the waters." In the age of law, water offered "a spiritual regeneration," Thomas said, "but it was imperfect and symbolic." This took place during the exodus from Egypt, when the waters parted and the Israelites passed through the Red Sea. (We can add many other incidents, as when Naaman the Syrian, a gentile, found healing by his sevenfold baptism in the Jordan River [see 2 Kgs 5:14].) Thus, according to St. Thomas, the Israelites saw "the mysteries of the kingdom of God, but only symbolically, 'seeing from afar' " (see Heb 11:13).

In the age of grace, however, the sign of water received its fullness, and now it works with divine power, "the power of the incarnate Word." Through baptism man is re-created, more truly born, "of water and the Holy Spirit" (Jn 3:5). In baptism, the "Israel of God" (Gal 6:16) passes through water to enter the promised land of heaven. These (and many more) Old Testament types find their fulfillment in the sacraments of the New Testament.

What applies to water applies to the other signs, as well. St. Thomas spoke also of "bread" in the three ages of salvation history. Bread has always provided sustenance for man in the order of nature; yet, in its "natural" state, it also prefigured the unleavened bread of the Passover and the manna that rained down in the desert. These in turn served as foreshadowing types of the Holy Eucharist, the Bread of Life (Jn 6:35–58). Thomas explained that each Old Testament type "is a symbol of the spiritual food. But they are different because [the manna] was only a symbol; while the other [the bread of the Christians] contains the thing that it symbolizes, that is, Christ Himself."

Aging Gracefully

God acts in a characteristic way. He reveals Himself according to a discernible pattern. He teaches in a way that respects human nature and human ways of knowing. Human beings know spiritual things by means of sensible things, since all our knowledge begins with sensory data. So, in order for us to understand what is spiritual in our rebirth, God conveyed it by sensible and material means.

In other words, throughout the ages of nature and law, God taught us as only God can, using things and events to signify still greater things and still mightier events.

In the fullness of time, however—in the age of grace—He sent His only Son. And it is in the age of grace that we live. Jesus Christ established the sacraments of the New Covenant, which elevate all that was sacramental in the ages of nature and law. Christ took up the signs of creation, culture, and the liturgy of Israel; "for," says the *Catechism,* "He Himself is the meaning of all these signs" (n. 1151). The sacraments of the Old Covenant had been many, and arduous, and weak against sin. Now, with the fullness of Christ's divine power, the sacraments of the New Covenant are fewer, and easier, and mighty against sin. In Christ, the sacraments found perfection and fulfillment.

Still, God does not override human nature in saving it. Indeed, in the age of grace, we come to receive supernatural realities by natural means, through sensible signs—and those signs are sacraments.

In the Old Covenant, we saw the kingdom of heaven "from afar." In the age of grace, we see that kingdom and its mysteries more clearly, but still imperfectly. It is only when we pass from the age of grace into the eternal age of glory that we'll see divine things as they really are, in heaven, without their earthly sacramental veils.

In heaven, St. Thomas said, "there is perfect regeneration . . . because we will be renewed both inwardly and outwardly. And therefore we shall see the kingdom of God in a most perfect way."

What will we "see" when God removes the sacramental veils of material water, for example? Water "ultimately signifies the grace of the Holy Spirit," St. Thomas said. "For the Holy Spirit is the unfailing fountain from whom all gifts of grace flow" (see Jn 7:37–39).

Water has served as a sacrament since the beginning of creation. Its meaning was partially disclosed in the age of law. And these types found fulfillment in the age of grace. Only in glory, however, may man gaze upon the reality signified by the sacraments. Only in heaven is the Living Water manifested apart from the sacramental veils—as the glory of the Spirit of God (see Rev 22:1).

CHAPTER 4

❧❦❧

As High
as Seven

ॐৎৎॐ

T HE CHURCH RECOGNIZES seven sacraments, no more, no less. They are: baptism, penance, Eucharist, confirmation, matrimony, holy orders, and the anointing of the sick.

From the days of the apostles, the Church has always celebrated these seven rites. In the early Church, however, the words "sacrament" and "mystery" were sometimes used indiscriminately to describe the sacraments instituted by Christ as well as other rituals and blessings. St. Augustine, for example, applied the word "sacrament" to many things, including the sign of the cross, the Bible, the practice of fasting, exorcism, and the blessing of salt (these are what we would today call "sacramentals"). Nevertheless, Augustine recognized the special role of the seven sacraments; and, in his work, we see the Church had already begun to reserve the term for those unique channels of grace that Jesus had established. By the Middle Ages, theologians commonly spoke of "the seven sacraments." The Council of Florence (1439) solemnly defined the number of sacraments as a dogma of faith. The Council of Trent (1545–1563) pronounced the dogma with an excommunication attached for anyone who rejected it.

Down through history and throughout the world, the sacramental rites have varied. In the East, for example, confirmation (called "chrismation") has almost always been administered immediately after baptism. The western Church, however, has been somewhat more mercurial, sometimes following the eastern custom, but most recently (and for many centuries) confirming believers later, in childhood or early adolescence.

Details may change. But the sacred sign, willed by Jesus Christ, remains constant. Thus, Christian marriage always involves one man and one woman, baptism always requires a washing in water accompanied by certain prayers.

Indeed, every sacrament involves both *words* and *actions* (see CCC, nn. 1153–1155). Traditionally, the Church has referred to these as "form" and "matter." And, for every sacrament, the Church designates an ordinary minister (and sometimes extraordinary ministers, too). We'll discuss the words, actions, and ministers of each sacrament in greater detail in just a moment.

Seven Wonders of the Word

For discussion's sake, we could divide the sacraments up in many ways. The Church fathers and popes and teachers provide many models. Most set the Eucharist over all as the

"Sacrament of sacraments." The Eucharist is different because, while the other sacraments are works of Jesus Christ, the Eucharist is Christ Himself—body, blood, soul, and divinity. The Eucharist, said the Second Vatican Council (1962–1965), is "the source and summit of the Christian life." "All the other sacraments," said St. Thomas Aquinas, "are ordered to it as to their end."

Once we have distinguished between the Eucharist and other sacraments, we may still further divide the sacraments for easier understanding. For the sake of simplicity and familiarity, we follow the threefold division used by most recent documents of the Church: the sacraments of initiation, the sacraments of healing, and the sacraments in service of communion.

The *sacraments of initiation* are baptism, confirmation, and Eucharist. These are the three sacraments that make a person a Christian—the sacraments that initiate someone into the Body of Christ.

The *sacraments of healing* are penance and the anointing of the sick. These two repair what is broken in the body and soul.

The *sacraments in service of communion* are marriage and holy orders. These sacraments build up the Church, in numbers and in strength; they are directed toward the good of others rather than oneself.

As we consider these rites one by one, I would like to speak of them in their proper context, and that is family life. For the Catholic Church is "nothing other than the family of God." In fact, the "family of God" is the *Cate-*

chism's favorite term for the Church (see n. 1655; also nn. 1, 542, 759, 854, 959, and 1632).

Each sacrament fulfills a particular function in God's family—a function that comes naturally to a good home and supernaturally to the home we call the Church.

Born to Win

BAPTISM

"By baptism we are reborn spiritually." Those are the very words of the Council of Florence. Christ Himself called us to be "born anew" "of water and the Spirit" (Jn 3:3, 5). St. Paul reveled in this "new creation" (2 Cor 5:17) and in our "adoption as sons" (Gal 4:5–7). By baptism, we become "partakers of the divine nature" (2 Pet 1:4); that is, we share God's very life.

Only by birth or adoption can we enjoy family life in a human household. Our birthright is to enjoy the guidance, discipline, and providence of human parents. Our parents have a duty to feed us and to foster our growth.

Born, adopted, created anew: By baptism we enter *God's family*. Only by baptism can we enjoy the fullness of life of God's household: the sharing of His table, His healing, His fatherly forgiveness and care. The early Christians saw the baptismal waters as the womb of the Church. As birth is a precondition of human family life, so baptism is the precondition of the other sacraments.

The essential action of baptism is the washing in

water—by pouring or immersion—accompanied by the words: "I baptize you in the name of the Father and of the Son and of the Holy Spirit" (Mt 28:19). The ordinary minister of baptism is a priest or deacon. But in case of emergency, such as the danger of imminent death, anyone can baptize validly, even a Buddhist, an atheist, or a Hindu. Even such extraordinary baptism corresponds to something in human family life. The newspapers regularly carry stories of pregnant women who find themselves suddenly in hard labor, far away from husband, midwife, or obstetrician. They have to make do with strangers and bystanders. The goal is a live birth, even into the hands of an "extraordinary minister." Afterward, and as soon as possible, the mother and child return to normal family and medical care. In the same way, a person baptized outside the normal rites of the Church should, at the first opportunity, be received into the Church by ordinary rites and instruction.

Baptism—like confirmation and holy orders—produces a permanent change in a person. These three sacraments, according to the Council of Florence, "imprint an indelible character on the soul, a kind of stamp that distinguishes it from the rest." Thus, these three sacraments can be received validly only once; they may never be repeated by the same person.

Baptism is a sign of birth and also a sign of washing. It cleanses the soul of all sins, sins actually committed, as well as original sin inherited from our first parents.

Olive the Above

CONFIRMATION

Some time after baptism, the Church confers a sacrament of strengthening. The word "firm" stands at the center of confirmation, and it is a "firming up" of the Christian. By baptism, we are born into the family. Through confirmation, God gives us the grace to reach Christian maturity within the family.

In the East, this sacrament is called "chrismation," after the oil of chrism that is applied during the rite. "Chrism" comes from the same word as "Christ": *Christos* is the Greek equivalent of the Hebrew "Messiah." Both words mean "anointed one." When we receive the chrism, we are anointed; we become like Christ; we become Christs. Christ Himself received His "anointing" from the Father, signified by the descent of the Holy Spirit (Jn 1:32). When Christ's redemptive work was complete, after His resurrection, He confirmed His disciples by giving them the Holy Spirit (Jn 20:22). In other words, the Father sent the Son to give us the Spirit. Christ gives us new life in baptism, but baptism is only the beginning. "Confirmation is necessary for the completion of baptismal grace" (CCC, n. 1285). In confirmation, we receive the fullness of the gift of the Holy Spirit.

Anointing symbolizes the passing on of power. The

Old and New Testaments are full of stories of anointing. Kings are anointed as they take the throne. Prophets receive anointing at the beginning of their ministry. Priests anoint successors for their work at the altar. These anointings are not merely ceremonial; they are efficacious, too— that is, they work wonders. One striking example is King Saul's anointing by the prophet Samuel (see 1 Sam 10:1–9). Afterward, Samuel explains, "the spirit of the Lord will come mightily upon you, and you shall prophesy . . . and be turned into another man" (v. 6). Immediately, the story relates, "God gave him [Saul] another heart" (v. 9).

For our biblical ancestors, olive oil held many powers: It was nourishing in food, a staple of the Mediterranean diet; it fueled the lamps that lit up family homes; it was the base of most medicines; it moistened skin dried out by desert climates; it soothed and loosened the limbs of athletes and soldiers. In God's family, the oils of the sacraments do all these things supernaturally. They give strength, light, nourishment, and healing.

The early Christians loved the sacrament of confirmation and called it by many poetic names: the laying on of hands (see Acts 8:17–18), the seal of the Lord, the stamp of the Lord. These are all images of fatherly love for a child reaching maturity. It is as if, in confirming us, God imprints us with the signet of the family. St. Paul said: "But it is God Who establishes us with you in Christ, and has commissioned us; He has put His seal upon us and given us His Spirit in our hearts as a guarantee" (1 Cor 1:21).

"The essential rite of confirmation is the laying on of

hands with anointing, accompanied by the words of the form" (see CCC, n. 1300). The ordinary minister of confirmation is a bishop or priest.

Mass Communication

EUCHARIST

Throughout this book, I discuss the Eucharist most of all the sacraments. In fact, I probably discuss the Eucharist as much as all the other sacraments combined, which is indeed just and right. Here I wish only to emphasize that it is the primary sacrament of nourishment in the family of God. The Mass is our family meal.

In Holy Communion, we receive the body and blood of Christ, and we "participate" in that body and blood (1 Cor 10:16). His presence is real and substantial. We share in His flesh and blood. We become what we eat. Together, we become "one body" in Christ (1 Cor 10:17), the mystical body of Christ (see Col 1:24, Eph 1:22–23).

At the family table, however, we do not merely feed our faces. St. Paul took to task the Corinthians who behaved in this way (1 Cor 11:22). The family table forms not only our bodies, but also our minds and souls. This is true of human homes, and it is also true of the household of God. Our "table talk" at the Mass includes plentiful readings from the Scriptures, and this is their privileged setting. Within the Mass, we receive special graces for understanding the Word of God. Remember the disciples on the first Easter Sunday who came to know Jesus "in the breaking of the bread" (Lk 24:35). It was in this context that He opened all the Scriptures up to them (Lk 24:33). It is in the Mass that the Scriptures are "actualized" for Christians today.

The Mass is the united worship of heaven and earth. It is the re-presentation of the one sacrifice of Jesus Christ on the cross. It is the real and abiding presence of Christ the King within His kingdom on earth, the Catholic Church. The riches of the Eucharist are unfathomable and inexhaustible.

The Church has many eucharistic liturgies, and they are rich in signs and symbols. The essential rite of the Eucharist is the eucharistic prayer, or canon, said by a validly ordained priest over the offerings of bread and wine.

The Absolution to Our Problems

PENANCE

This sacrament goes by many names today, most popularly "the sacrament of reconciliation" and "confession." It is the sacrament by which Christ forgives our sins through the absolution of the priest.

The most ancient manual of the Church's sacramental and moral life, the *Didache,* urged Christians to confess their sins before approaching the altar for Communion. It is, after all, by confessing our sins and receiving forgiveness that we are restored to normal family life.

The classic expression of Jesus' doctrine of confession and forgiveness is a family story. It is the story of the prodigal son (Lk 15:11–32). In that parable, we see the drama of sin, repentance, confession, forgiveness, and restoration to the family table. All the elements are there, allegorically describing the life Jesus would leave for His Church. We are sons of almighty God; but we stray; and so He humbles Himself to come down to us and give us what we need to come home to stay.

Jesus did not leave us orphans. He prepared His apostles to act as fathers in the Church. As fathers, they would forgive, like the father of the prodigal son; and, as fathers, they would help their children to get scrubbed and properly clothed for the family meal. Jesus said to Simon Peter: "I will give you the keys to the kingdom of heaven, and whatever you bind on earth shall be bound in heaven, and whatever you loose on earth shall be loosed in heaven" (Mt 16:19). Jesus told all the apostles: "If you forgive the sins of any, they are forgiven; if you retain the sins of any, they are retained" (Jn 20:23).

The apostles took Him at His word and extended that ministry to the penitents of their early congregations. St. James urged his hearers to "confess your sins to one another, and pray for one another, that you may be healed" (Jas 5:16). The context is key to our understanding this passage. James is not saying that *anyone* can administer the sacrament of confession. He speaks of this particular ministry among the duties of the "elders of the Church" (v. 14). The Greek word for "elders" is *presbuteroi,* from which we derive the English "priest." The ordinary minister of the sacrament of penance is a priest or bishop.

Celebration of the sacrament varies widely from time to time and place to place. Certain elements are essential. First, the person approaching the sacrament must be sorry; he must confess his sins; and he must perform the act of penance prescribed by the priest. The priest pronounces the words of absolution ("I absolve you . . ."), prays for the sinner, and does penance with him (see CCC, n. 1448).

Heaven and Health

ANOINTING OF THE SICK

The sign of anointing here expresses healing and consolation. Anointing strengthens the spirit of someone who is suffering, but it also commends them to Christ, "that He may raise them up and save them." This anointing extends Christ's healing touch (see CCC, n. 1504). The sacrament *always* heals in the way Christ intends. Sometimes it brings about a physical cure or relief of symptoms. Most times it heals by empowering the sick to suffer like Christ. Anointed, we are "other christs"; and we must never forget that Christ Himself suffered and died. Scripture tells us that the perfect Man—who, like a pioneer, blazed our trail to salvation—was made "perfect through suffering" (Heb 2:10). In our suffering, Christ draws us closer to Himself in His sufferings on the cross. And we are made perfect!

"My grace is sufficient for you," He told St. Paul. "My power is made perfect in weakness" (2 Cor 12:9). Like St. Paul, the anointed Christian can say: "I complete what is lacking in Christ's afflictions for the sake of His body, that is, the Church" (Col 1:24). Our suffering works as reparation for our own sins and, like Christ's, for the salvation of other members of God's family.

In most of the world and through much of history, healing has been a family affair. The family tends to its sick members, treats them, feeds them, administers the medicines, and applies the ointments. In most of the world and through much of history, people died at home, in their beds. Their families prepared their bodies for burial by anointing.

By sacramental anointing, the Church heals us and prepares us for the ultimate healing of our bodies at the resurrection.

St. James gives us the Bible's most explicit and eloquent record of this sacrament: "Is any among you sick? Let him call for the elders of the Church and let them pray over him, anointing him with oil in the name of the Lord; and the prayer of faith will save the sick man, and the Lord will raise him up; and if he has committed sins, he will be forgiven" (Jas 5:14–15). Again, in this passage, the "elders" are the priests (from the Greek: *presbuteroi*). The priests are the ordinary ministers of the rite, which consists of anointing the sick person with oil blessed by the bishop.

This sacrament is often administered along with penance and the Eucharist, especially for those who are gravely ill or dying. The *Catechism* (n. 1525) compares this awesome threesome to the three sacraments of initiation. As we come into God's earthly home by the power of baptism, confirmation, and Eucharist, so we proceed to His heavenly home by the power of anointing, penance, and Eucharist, collectively called the "last rites" or "last sacraments."

Fathers of the Church

HOLY ORDERS

Through ordination, God raises up fathers for His earthly family, the Church. Holy orders is the sacrament by which men receive the power and grace to perform the sacred duties of bishops, priests, and other ministers of the Church. Jesus instituted the sacrament at the Last Supper when He gave His Apostles the power and the duty to say Mass, to "Do this in remembrance of Me." After His resurrection, He breathed on them and gave them the power to forgive sins. By His command, He enabled them to heal in His name (see Mt 10:8).

Throughout the Bible, priests appear as spiritual fathers. In the Book of Genesis, priestly paternity is explicit. In the beginning, there is no separate priestly caste. Family and church are one. Houses are domestic sanctuaries, meals are sacrifices, hearths are altars—all because fathers are empowered as priests by nature. Each father passes on his priesthood to his firstborn son.

This practice continues until Israel sins grievously by worshipping the golden calf. At that point, God confines the priesthood to the Levites, the only tribe that remained faithful to Him. Yet, even then, the people of Israel looked to their priests as fathers. In the Book of Judges, when a Levite appeared at Micah's door, Micah pleads, "Stay with me, and be to me a father and a priest" (Jg 17:10). A chapter later, Micah's plea is echoed, almost verbatim, by the Danites as they invite the Levite to be priest for their entire tribe: "Come with us, and be to us a father and a priest" (Jg 18:19).

In the fullness of time, God the Father sent Jesus as a faithful firstborn son (Heb 1:6) and a priest (Heb 10:21)—not only to restore the natural priesthood, but also to establish a supernatural priesthood within the divine family, the Church.

That is the priesthood exercised by Christ through the apostles. In turn, the apostles ordained priests, bishops, and deacons to succeed them (see Acts 14:23, 20:17; Phil 1:1; Tit 1:5–9). We see it today as bishops lay hands upon priests and pronounce the words of consecration—the essential rite of ordination. Only a bishop can validly ordain a man as priest.

How does a priest "father" the family of the Church? Think of the ways an ordinary dad fathers his natural children. Fathers give life. They nurture life. As breadwinners, they care for it. They instruct. They raise that life to maturity. In an analogous way, priests give life through baptism; they nourish their spiritual offspring through the Eucharist; they discipline through penance; they instruct through their preaching; they raise their congregations to full Christian maturity as contributing members of God's family.

Then Comes Marriage

MATRIMONY

Nowhere is the "family connection" so evident as in the sacrament of matrimony. For it is matrimony that makes new Christian homes, which tradition calls "domestic churches." Matrimony is the sacrament by which a baptized man and a baptized woman bind themselves for life in a lawful marriage and receive the grace to fulfill the duties of the married state.

The Bible presents marriage as the primary metaphor for the union of God and His people, Christ and the Church. This theme recurs in the Old Testament, and it finds its fullest expression in the fifth chapter of St. Paul's Letter to the Ephesians: "A man shall leave his father and mother and be joined to his wife, and the two shall become one flesh" (Eph 5:31). St. Paul goes on to say: "This mystery is a profound one, and I am saying that it refers to Christ and the Church" (v. 32). Paul's word for mystery, *mysterion,* is the early Church's preferred term for "sacrament"; in fact, in this passage, it was translated into Latin as *sacramentum.*

Christ has married the Church, indissolubly and eternally. He has given His own life for her life, and that makes matrimony a sacrament. Prior to the coming of Christ, marriage was a natural phenomenon and even a covenanted union; but it became a sacrament of grace only when Christ established a new family order in His own flesh and blood with the Church as his bride and very body (for the two become "one flesh").

Thus, every sacramental marriage becomes, as it were, a homily, a message, an icon of the union between Christ and His Church.

The free consent of a man and woman is what constitutes the sacrament. As soon as a couple expresses and exchanges consent, they have ratified their covenant. But the *sacrament* of matrimony becomes purely and absolutely indissoluble only when that marriage is consummated through the act of marriage: that is, sexual intercourse.

Matrimony is ratified by vows and consummated by sexual union. Thus, the ministers of the sacrament of marriage are the husband and wife. Ordinarily, for validity, a priest or deacon will preside at the exchange of vows and "witness" on behalf of the Church.

Christ made marriage a sacrament of His total, unbreakable, and abundantly fruitful communion with the Church. That is why the Church has always forbidden divorce, polygamy, birth control, abortion, sodomy, and other practices that destroy matrimony's power to signify God's love.

What are the effects of the sacrament? Like all sacraments, matrimony brings about an increase in sanctifying grace; that is, even apart from your spouse, you are joined closer to Jesus Christ. You receive a greater fullness of the Holy Spirit (see CCC, n. 1624). You mature as a child of God. Then you receive a special sacramental grace that enables you to love with a divine love, to love as Christ loves, to forgive as Christ forgives. For, unless a couple is willing to live like Him, love like Him, and forgive like Him, their marriage will not work (see CCC, n. 1609).

In God We Trust

The sacraments have a fixed number, and their celebration follows ritual forms that incorporate certain prescribed actions and materials. Their administration is reserved to certain ministers. And, in the end, they always bestow God's grace.

Nevertheless, they are not mechanical processes or magical manipulations. The sacraments of the New Covenant contain the grace they signify and they bestow it on those who do not hinder it. That is God's work, pure and simple.

The primary minister of all the sacraments is Christ Himself. Moreover, it is Christ Himself Who produces their effect in our souls. In other words, even the human ministers are Christ's instruments for giving His life to His loved ones.

This is no magical manipulation of God. It is, rather,

God's lavish gift of His life to His family. Approaching it from our side, we see the sacraments as the humble submission of God's children to the words and the works that their heavenly Father has established for the good of His family.

CHAPTER 5

❦❧

WHAT'S THE BIG IDEA?

The Meaning of Covenant
(and Everything Else)

W HEN WE TALK about the sacraments, we can't help but come back, again and again, to a single short phrase. The *Catechism of the Catholic Church* uses the same phrase to describe the ancient liturgies of Israel and of the Church. So do the great rabbis of Judaism. In fact, it is the phrase used by the Old Testament itself.

The liturgies of ancient Israel, like the liturgies of the Catholic Church, are "signs of the covenant."

Signs of the covenant: The words come readily to mind for both popes and rabbis; and, to most ordinary people, they seem so plain that they can be safely glossed over. But it's really not safe to do that. For there is no idea more important to Scripture—and no idea more important to your life—than the idea of *covenant*. And the covenant cannot be understood apart from its divinely appointed signs.

We've already examined the sacraments as "signs," and we've seen that God's signs are more than mere words or symbols. They are realities, events, and life. Now let's turn to the second key term in that phrase: *covenant*.

An I for a You

Most people think they know what the word "covenant" means. In modern legal jargon, it's a kind of contract. Some dictionaries even treat "covenant" as a synonym for "contract." But such usage will not help us when we try to understand the Bible. For the ancient Israelites had a word for contract *(hozeh),* and they had a word for covenant *(berith)*—and the two were in no sense inter-changeable.

Contracts usually exchange property, goods, and services. But covenants exchange persons. Contracts set the terms for a business transaction. But covenants create a family bond. Every covenant is based upon a contract, since all interpersonal relationships involve some sharing of property and obligations of service. Still, a covenant extends far beyond the limits of any contract. When people enter into a covenant, they say, "I am yours, and you are mine." Thus, marriage is a covenant, and adoption is a covenant.

To the biblical authors (and to most ancient peoples), the difference between covenant and contract was like the difference between marriage and prostitution, or between adoption and slavery.

God's relationship with man is a covenant; and "cove-

nant" is the only word that will do to describe it. God
Himself said: "I will establish My covenant with you"
(Gen 6:18; see also Gen 17:21 and Ex 6:4). For God is not
merely demanding certain behaviors and prohibiting
others, in return for specified rewards and punishments.
God's covenant is not a mere contract; He is not only ex-
changing property, goods, or services. God's covenant is an
exchange of persons: "You shall be My people, and I will
be your God" (Ezek 36:28).

Covenants constitute families. God made His covenants in order to establish or renew a family bond with human beings, whom He has created in His own image.

First Will and Testament

Covenant is, quite arguably, the most important concept
in the Bible. This is evident even in the division of the
Scriptures. We say that the Bible is made up of two "Testaments," the Old and the New. "Testament" comes from
the Latin word *testamentum,* which St. Jerome used to
translate the Greek and Hebrew words for covenant:
diatheke and *berith,* respectively. If custom counted for
nothing, we could more accurately say that our Bibles
are divided into the "Old Covenant" and the "New
Covenant."

And it's true: Even in the days of the Old Covenant,
the prophets spoke of the day when God would establish a
"New Covenant" (Jer 31:31), an "everlasting covenant"
(Jer 32:40). In the fullness of time, Jesus declared this

prophecy fulfilled by His own saving work: "This . . . is the New Covenant in my blood" (Lk 22:20). The earliest Christians used those crucial terms as a title for their Lord: "Jesus, the mediator of a New Covenant" (Heb 12:24).

Covenant, then, is the defining feature of God's relations with humankind. It is the law undergirding all divine law. It is the principle that guides the course of all human events. If we understand the covenant, we can see not only how events unfold in biblical history, but we can also see why they unfold the way they do. The history of Israel is the history of God fathering His family, the chosen people—whose every member has been sacramentally incorporated into God's assembly.

St. Paul, when writing in Greek, used a certain term to speak of God's fatherly plan for creation. He called it God's *oikonomia*—his "plan for the fullness of time" (Eph 1:10; see also CCC, n. 236). The closest English equivalent to *oikonomia* is "economy," though current usage doesn't convey the word's theological freight. In Greek, the word means, literally, "law of the household," "law of the home and family."

By covenants, God created and renewed a family bond with His people. He did this, as we have said before, in a characteristic way, by outward signs. "Now even the first covenant had regulations for worship and an earthly sanctuary" (Heb 9:1). From the beginning of time, God made covenants with His people, and He taught them how to seal and renew those covenants liturgically. The rituals were, in every case, essential to the relationship; and indeed, they were often treated as equivalent to the covenant, for they were divinely established "signs of the covenant."

Modern people will often speak of worship as something outside the stream of history—purely transcendent. Not so the ancients: They knew no distinction between the sacred and the secular. The covenant was an exchange of persons, and so it comprehended all of life: private, public, professional, religious, recreational, everything. The idea of a Sunday-only Christian—or a Sabbath-only Jew—would be ludicrous to our ancestors in biblical faith.

The covenant rites, then, did not require God's people to remove themselves from the swift current of history. The rites themselves were, rather, the channel through which the stream of history flowed.

Israel's worship was the driving force in history, and so it is carefully and minutely recorded in the sacred books.

The Rest of the Story

When God gave the law to Moses, He revealed how, from the beginning of time, He had built creation itself as a Temple, with its own liturgical cycle, with its own "sign" of the covenant between God and the human race: "You shall keep My sabbaths, for this is a sign between Me and you throughout your generations, that you may know that I, the Lord, sanctify you. . . . It is a sign forever between Me and the people of Israel that in six days the Lord made heaven and earth, and on the seventh day He rested, and was refreshed" (Ex 31:13, 17). The Sabbath, then, is the outward sign of God's covenant with creation, and specifically with Adam, with mankind. The Lord pledged to "sanctify" those who keep this primal liturgy. To observe the Sabbath, then, was to keep the covenant (see Is 56:6). Here, as elsewhere, God's people commonly equated the sign with the signified, the sacrament with the covenant.

In describing later generations, the Bible presents the rites of the covenant in greater detail, and the liturgies grow more elaborate; but the sacred writers rarely provide commentary or interpretation of the rites. It's not that they're trying to hide anything; they're not deliberately trying to keep things obscure, as did the fabricators of later "mystery religions." Rather, the sacred authors seem to assume an intimate knowledge of covenants and their terms, forms, and consequences.

There was good reason for this. For every reader or hearer of the Scriptures—indeed, for every man, woman, and child in the ancient world—all of life was shaped by covenants. These pacts determined not only a person's relations with God, but with others, as well. Covenant was much more important than blood relation in determining membership in a family. Indeed, it was the legal, ritual means of welcoming new family members, and it was the ordinary, periodic way for established family members to renew their bonds.

Everything else in life depended upon the relationship established in the covenant ritual. As scholar Walter Bruggemann put it: "in the world of biblical faith, the family is the primary unit of meaning which shapes and defines reality." If you were a citizen of ancient Israel—or even Assyria, Greece, or Rome—covenants defined your relationships with others, your choice of a profession, your role in society. It determined whom you married and where you lived.

For ancient people, the world was defined by the family, the tribe, the clan. Covenant was what placed you inside or cast you outside that "world." There was no place for individualism in the ancient world. Indeed, when nations struck a treaty, they inevitably sealed it with a covenant expressed in the language of the family, as a marriage or an adoption.

We are fortunate that a good number of these "lesser" covenant documents have survived. For they cast light on what the biblical writers leave unexplained when they describe the ancient liturgies.

Whether they were designed to seal treaties, marriages, or adoptions, the covenants often shared certain common elements. Both parties to the covenant would (1) solemnly swear a sacred oath, (2) offer a sacrifice, and (3) share a common meal. Though these three actions do not appear (at least explicitly) in all covenants, they appear frequently enough—in biblical and other sources—to demand our careful study. Indeed, these three elements often constitute the traditional signs of the covenants—the sacraments of the Old Covenant and of the New.

Taking God at His Word

To understand the oaths of our ancestors, we need to un-learn the common usage of the word today. Modern people tend to treat the words "oath," "vow," and "promise" as virtually synonymous. They're not.

When I make a promise, I give my word, my name, my signature. People sometimes seal promises with the phrase "on my honor," meaning that they offer their own reputation as surety; they risk their own standing in the community. If they prove to be lying or derelict in their duty, their name is devalued, and perhaps their family's name, as well.

A vow is more weighty than an ordinary promise, be-cause it is a promise made directly to God. When we make a vow, we give *God* our word.

When people swear an oath, however, they place much more at stake. An oath is "the invocation of *God's name* as a witness to truth" (*Code of Canon Law,* can. 1199.1). An oath is based upon a promise; but people who swear an oath seal their promise with the words "by God," or "in God's name," "so help me, God," or something sim-ilar. When God's name is used in an oath, He becomes an active partner in the transaction. Those who swear place not their own honor at risk, but God's honor. The *Cate-chism* puts it well: "When it is truthful and legitimate, an oath highlights the relationship of human speech with

God's truth. A false oath calls on God to be witness to a lie" (CCC, n. 2151).

To swear falsely is to commit a most serious sin, and to do it, explicitly, in God's name. False oaths trigger the most dire consequences. Even in secular legal systems, perjury under oath is punished severely. God is no less exacting. We read in the prophet Ezekiel: "Because he despised the oath and broke the covenant, . . . he shall not escape. Therefore thus says the Lord God: As I live, surely My oath which he despised, and My covenant which he broke, I will requite upon his head" (Ezek 17:18–19).

This manner of judgment is built into the ancient understanding of oaths. For our ancestors, every oath carried both blessings and curses—blessings upon the fulfillment of the oath, but curses if it were broken. God made this clear in the classic formulation of His covenant with Israel: "I call heaven and earth to witness against you this day, that I have set before you life and death, blessing and curse; therefore choose life, that you and your descendants may live, loving the Lord your God, obeying His voice, and cleaving to Him; for that means life to you and length of days, that you may dwell in the land which the Lord swore to your fathers" (Dt 30:19–20).

Whoever takes up this covenant must take the oath, its form, its terms, and its consequences. Here God plainly states both the blessings and the curses.

Not always, however, were the ancient oaths made verbally explicit. Sometimes the oath and its consequences were symbolized by a wordless, physical sign, an *oath-in-action,* as when Israelites circumcised their sons.

A Cut of the Action

The act of sacrifice could mean many things to the people we meet in the Bible. It was a recognition of God's sovereignty over creation: "The earth is the Lord's" (Ps 24:1). Man acknowledged this fact by giving back to God what is ultimately His.

A sacrifice could also be an act of thanksgiving. Creation is given to man as a gift, but what return can man make to God (see Ps 116:12)? We can only give back what we ourselves have received.

Sacrifice could also serve as an outward sign of sorrow for one's sins. The person offering sacrifice recognized that his sins deserved death; he offered the animal's life in place of his own.

But, most important, sacrifice signified the sealing of a covenant. The Lord said: "Gather to Me my faithful ones, who made a covenant with Me by sacrifice" (Ps 50:5).

When offered in the context of a covenant oath, a sacrifice implied something truly ominous. Consider Abraham's sacrifice to God in Genesis 15. God tells Abraham, "Bring Me a heifer three years old, a she-goat three years old, a ram three years old, a turtledove, and a young pigeon" (v. 9). Abraham obeys and brings the animals forward; then, without a word of explanation, he proceeds to "cut them in two, and laid each half over against the other" (v. 10).

What's going on here? What can be the meaning of this strange mutilation?

This was the most common ritual form for sealing a covenant. Evidence abounds from the ancient Israelites, Hittites, and Greeks. Indeed, this practice explains the origin of the Hebrew phrase "to cut a covenant."

Some anthropologists assign religious ritual to the realm of the irrational and illogical. But that is wrongheaded. These bloody rites of sacrifice manifest reason and logic that even Socrates and Plato had to recognize.

Rabbi Nahum Sarna brings out what is implicit in every "cutting" of a covenant: "It is generally believed that when the contracting parties passed between the severed pieces they thereby accepted the covenant obligations and invoked upon themselves the fate of the animals if the terms of the pact were violated." In other words, they were saying with their bodies: "If I am unfaithful to my covenant oath, may I suffer the same fate as this mutilated beast."

The covenant sign of circumcision served a similar purpose. It was a small cutting of an important and sensitive organ, and it symbolized still greater consequences: the failure of the generative power, an end to a family's line of descendants.

When Abraham "cut" these covenants, he knew what he was taking upon himself—and his countless descendants, among whom we Christians count ourselves.

Meal Bonding

The parties of a covenant usually ratified their pact with an oath and a blood sacrifice. But the sacrifice was not complete until the sacrificial victim was consumed. This third and last action—the consuming of the victim—signified the purpose and goal of the sacrifice. For God Himself had ordained and commanded sacrifices in the Old Covenant, but not simply so that animals would be killed. The killing was penultimate. After the animals were killed, they were eaten in a common meal.

To share that meal, to share familial communion, was the purpose and goal of the sacrifice. It signified the forging or the restoration of family bonds. With whom did individuals eat almost all their daily meals? With their family members.

The common meal is so clearly important to the ancient covenants, and so often found in sources outside the Bible, that some scholars have proposed that the word *berith* derives from a more ancient Semitic word meaning "meal."

Whether or not "meal" is the root of covenant, it is certainly the fruit of the covenant bond. It is the fitting conclusion to the familial covenant between Jacob and Laban (Gen 32:44, 54). It is the very stuff of the Passover liturgy: the seder meal. There, as elsewhere, the meal was not optional. Indeed, those who did not eat the paschal lamb would awake to find their firstborn dead. Similarly, the Sinai covenant concluded with Israel's chosen leaders consuming a meal in God's presence: "they beheld God, and ate and drank" (Exod 24:11). Indeed, many rabbis have interpreted the entire sacrificial system of the Jerusalem Temple as a code of etiquette for eating sacred meals in God's presence.

All of these Old Covenant meals hinted at some aspect of the sacred meal of the New Covenant. The ancient types of the meal found their fulfillment and perfection in the Mass, which Jesus established at the Last Supper. At that Passover seder, Jesus explicitly made the connection between His meal and the New Covenant (Mt 26:28). St. Paul showed that the meal of Jesus' body and blood marked the beginning of a new celebration for a new covenant: "Christ, our Passover, has been sacrificed for us, therefore, let us keep the feast" (1 Cor 5:7). What feast? The Eucharistic banquet, the covenant Passover. The ancient Christians did not even bother to change the name of the feast day. Even today, in most languages other than English and German, some variant of "Pesach" remains the term to denote both Passover and Easter.

Jesus established forever a meal in God's presence—His *real presence,* for the Eucharist is the "Lord's supper" (1 Cor 11:20).

Unless Is More

If we come to a truly biblical understanding of the covenant and its sacraments, we will see why the earliest Christians spoke of the Mass as "the sacrifice," sealed with the blood of Christ. We will see also why the Church has always celebrated the feast with the meal of bread and wine. And we will see why so many of the earliest Christian liturgies were cast in the form of sworn oaths.

After all that, it should be radiantly clear why Jesus mandated His sacramental oath, sacrifice, and meal. Note his repeated use of the word "unless": "unless one is born of water and the Spirit, he cannot enter the kingdom of God" (Jn 3:5) . . . "unless you eat of the flesh of the Son of man and drink His blood, you have no life in you" (Jn 6:53).

These terms of the covenant apply just as much to us today as they applied to our ancestors in the faith—whether Abraham at Moriah, Moses at Sinai, or Paul in Corinth.

When we take the sacraments, we make a covenant. Like Abraham walking between the severed animals, we should go in to each liturgy fully aware of the possible consequences. We should know and believe the terms of the oath we're swearing. We should remain aware of the covenant's curses, so that we'll enjoy the covenant's blessings.

CHAPTER 6

❀❦❀

DO YOU
SOLEMNLY SWEAR?

Sacraments as
Covenant Oaths

THE FIRST WEDDING I ever attended was my own. So the words of my vows struck me as not only powerful, but fresh, new, and uniquely mine: "I promise, before God and these witnesses, to be your loving and faithful husband; in plenty and in want; in joy and in sorrow; in sickness and in health; as long as we both shall live."

I could not know it at the time, but by making a vow and invoking God by name, I was fulfilling the Catholic Church's definition of an oath. Nor could I know that I was, by that very action, celebrating a sacrament of the New Covenant—a sacrament of the Catholic Church. The Calvinist tradition, to which I subscribed, has never recognized matrimony as a sacrament.

Yet a sacrament it remains, whether or not a couple recognize it as such. An oncoming truck remains a truck even if a pedestrian doesn't see it, and he will feel its impact if he stands in its way.

Sacraments are more real than any tractor trailer, and they arrive with far greater impact.

From Love to Law

As surely as Abraham, I swore an oath. As surely as any bishop or priest, I celebrated a sacrament. All this took place not because of my piety or my knowledge of doctrine. It took place *ex opere operato* (by the very fact of the work's being performed)—by the power of God's grace.

Ex opere operato: what a strange and wonderful phrase. And it is true not just because it is Catholic doctrine; it is Catholic doctrine because it is true. Even secularist societies recognize that the rite of marriage changes a couple, and it imposes on them a host of obligations. Once we pronounce those wedding vows—and by the very act of pronouncing those vows—we subject ourselves to the thousands of ordinances that fill hundreds of volumes of family law, at the local, state, federal, and even international level.

As surely as Abraham placed himself between the entrails of sacrificial beasts, Kimberly and I knelt between our parents and future in-laws, and we accepted the terms of the marriage covenant.

For us as for every bride and groom, those vows required an enormous act of faith. No one goes into marriage entirely prepared for what's ahead. Married life is full of surprises. But our common degree of ignorance (the human condition) does not exempt us from the duties of family life or our obligation to be faithful to the marriage covenant. Marriage vows include no contingency clause, and they demand fidelity no matter what delights or disasters come our way: plenty or want, joy or sorrow, sickness or health.

The minister witnessed to the truth, on that late-summer afternoon in 1979, as he recited the customary prayer over our rings: "By Your blessing, O God, may these rings be to Scott and Kimberly symbols of unending love and faithfulness, reminding them of the covenant they have made this day, through Jesus Christ our Lord. Amen."

Swearing Like a Soldier

When we make a covenant, we bind ourselves to live by a divinely ordered law. Sometimes Christians think of "law" as something that belongs exclusively to the Old Covenant. But Jesus Himself tells us, "Truly I say to you, till heaven and earth pass away, not an iota, not a dot, will pass from the law until all is accomplished" (Mt 5:18). Jesus did not abolish the law; rather, He held His followers to a higher standard than even the most scrupulous observance of the law of Moses (see Mt 5:20).

A covenant binds two parties together as family, and every household requires a certain order. Every family lives with some degree of protocol, etiquette, and manners, or they do not live in peace. The law of the covenant—whether it be God's covenant with Noah, Moses, or Jesus—spells out the conditions of living in the family of God.

The Israelites knew this. The earliest Christians knew this. What's more, their pagan contemporaries knew it, too. In the writings of a pagan Roman, we find the earliest and most fascinating convergence of the notions of oath, law, and sacrament.

Pliny the Younger was a Roman imperial official whose life overlapped with the lives of the apostles. Around the year 112, he was serving as governor of Bithynia (in what is now Turkey), and he filed a report with the emperor describing the problems he faced in the emerging cult of the Christians. Working from surveillance and interrogations, Pliny described the Sunday worship of Christians: "They were in the habit of meeting on a certain fixed day before it was light, and they sang in alternate verses a hymn to Christ, as to a god, and bound themselves by a solemn oath, not to any wicked deeds, but never to commit any fraud, theft or adultery, never to falsify their word, nor deny a trust when they should be called upon to deliver it up. Afterward, it was their custom to . . . partake of food, but food of an ordinary and innocent kind."

Pliny didn't know quite what he was dealing with. But his Christian subjects might have explained that the ritual in question was the Mass, and the "ordinary" food was the Eucharist.

But what about Pliny's curious observation that members of the congregation "bound themselves by a solemn oath"? What does the Mass have do do with an oath?

Perhaps the answer is to be found in the Latin word

that Pliny used to describe the oath. He called it a *sacramentum*—from which we have derived the English word "sacrament." We do not know whether Pliny was merely relaying the term that the Christians used to describe their liturgy, or whether he was imposing his own interpretation on the rites. Either way, his choice of the word *sacramentum*—with his observation about its binding effects—is illuminating.

For the term *sacramentum* was commonplace in the Latin of Pliny's generation, and it had a precise meaning. The *sacramentum* was the sacred oath sworn by men on entering the Roman military. Listen to the way one scholar describes the effects of that oath:

> *This swearing of the* sacramentum *changed the status of the man entirely. He was now utterly subject to his general's authority, and had thereby laid down any restraints of his former civilian life. His actions would be by the will of the general. . . . There was more than mere practicality behind the change from the white toga of the citizen to the blood red tunic of the legionary. The symbolism was such that the blood of the vanquished would not stain him. He was now no longer a citizen whose conscience would not allow for murder. Now he was a soldier. The legionary could only be released from the* sacramentum *by two things: death or demobilization. Without the* sacramentum, *however, the Roman could not be a soldier.*

What was the Roman *sacramentum*? It was the most sacred of oaths. It was life-changing. It involved an outward sign of an invisible reality. It subjected the will of the individual to the will of another person. It subjected the recruit to a new law. The word *sacramentum* was sometimes used to describe other oaths, but always with the same degree of binding power and gravity.

The *sacramentum* was, in the gentile world, the virtual equivalent to the *covenant* oaths of Israel. When it came to describing the rituals of the Christians, Pliny used the most precise term the Latin language could supply.

Pliny's usage was surely not accidental; nor was it unique. Two generations later, the empire's greatest attorney converted to Christianity. His name was Tertullian, and he lived in North Africa. Tertullian was a prolific writer whose works betray a lingering attachment to the terminology of the Roman legal system. He is especially fond of the word *sacramentum,* and he uses it many times, clearly intending all of the following meanings: an oath, a sign, a rite of the Church, baptism, the Eucharist, and the foreshadowings found in the Old Covenant.

The pagan Pliny and the Christian Tertullian were poles apart in their attitudes toward the Christian Church. Both, however, were brilliant lawyers. Both spoke with precision and care. And both could see that the Christian mysteries were best understood as sacraments—that is, as sacred oaths that sealed, renewed, and signified membership in a covenant family.

Terms of Endearment

Most people will find it easy to see the similarity between the ancient *sacramentum* and the Christian sacrament of marriage. In both, there are vows, a change in family affiliation, and so on. But in what way could the *sacramentum* possibly correspond to the Eucharist or baptism? What did Pliny and Tertullian see so easily that we moderns see only with difficulty?

After all, when, in our day and age, has anyone ever stopped the Mass and, like a bailiff in a courtroom, administered an oath to the congregation? Could it be that the "oath" was just an oddity of the churches in second-century Bithynia and third-century Africa?

The simple answer to this last question is: no. The meaning of the Mass has not changed since the days of the late Roman Empire, and neither has the binding power of the sacramental oath. Moreover, we continue, today, to pray the Mass using the ancient forms of covenant oaths and the *sacramentum*.

"An oath engages the Lord's name," says the *Catechism of the Catholic Church* (n. 2150), and that is what we do at the beginning of every Mass. We trace the sign of the cross over our bodies as we pray: "In the *name* of the Father, and of the Son, and of the Holy Spirit." Then we conclude that invocation with the same word the ancient Hebrews used to express their solemn acceptance of a covenant oath: "amen," meaning "yes," or "I do," or "so be it." "Amen" was a common oath formula in Israel (see Num 5:22). And the ancient rabbis ruled that every blessing must meet with the response of "amen" in order to make it legally valid.

In the introductory rites, then, we have engaged the Lord's name and consented to the terms of the covenant. Every Mass is an oath "sworn" in God's name.

To what terms do we give our consent? We plead guilty to our sins in the penitential rite. We accept as binding "the Word of the Lord" in the Scripture readings of the Mass. We pledge to accept and obey all Catholic teaching when we profess in the creed that "We believe in one holy, catholic, and apostolic Church." We swear to live the truth, the whole truth, and nothing but the truth. As Pliny might put it: Catholics bind themselves by a solemn oath not to do any wicked deeds; and they bind themselves to Christ "as to a god."

Order in the Court

Every liturgical event is a juridical event as well. Every Catholic church is, in a sense, a courthouse, where the chosen people swear their covenant oath to live as God's family.

This, perhaps, will offend modern sensibilities. We are accustomed to the strict separation of church and state, and so we have placed the "liturgical" and the "legal" in separate, watertight categories. But such a separation would be nonsense to our ancestors in the faith. For the Israelites and the early Christians, religion and law were inseparable, and they were family matters, concerning those who were kin by covenant in the family of God.

Nor was this a peculiarly Judeo-Christian notion. In the ancient world, it was universally human. When the Romans persecuted Christians, they demanded two things from them: sacrifices and oaths. The emperors knew that to overturn one covenant, to nullify one *sacramentum,* the swearing of another was required. So they tested those accused of Christianity by demanding that they swear by the emperor (as a god) or by the emperor's "genius" (his protector god).

The Roman oaths were similar to those of the Israelites. They promised similar terms, similar blessings and curses: life for those who fulfilled the terms of the oath, death for those who did not. "I swear by the genius of Caesar Vespasian Augustus that my statement is true. May I prosper if I have sworn truly and the opposite if I have sworn falsely."

Such were the words by which some Christians committed apostasy. Others, by refusing to swear, gained the martyrs' crown. Two second-century martyrs of Lyons, Blandina and Ponticus—like many other Christians—suffered torture and death precisely because they refused to "swear . . . by idols."

Nor was the imperial cult the only religious oath that bound the empire's people to false gods. The immensely popular Mithras brotherhood and other "mystery cults" did the same.

The Christian Church considered these oaths binding and covenantal, though sworn in the name of false gods. It was assumed, in those days, that most of the people who approached the baptismal font would be bound by such covenants "and all their empty promises." This was the original purpose of the "renunciation of Satan" that remains in the baptismal vows even today. The great fourth-century bishop of Jerusalem, St. Cyril, told his class of converts: "When you renounce Satan, you trample underfoot your entire covenant with him, and abrogate your former treaty with hell."

The word applied to this rite of renunciation speaks volumes. Today we call it "exorcism," from the Greek words *ex horkizein*—literally, to "oath out." The New Covenant "oaths out" all the old covenants that bind unbelievers.

Under Protection of the Law

In baptism, in the Mass, at our marriage, and in every sacrament we celebrate, we invoke the name of the Lord, and we bind ourselves by covenant oath. We swear not by our own name, but by God's. We swear not on our own honor, but on God's. We call upon the Church as our witness. We pledge ourselves to obey the Word of God, as revealed in Scripture and Tradition. We accept the blessings that come with our fidelity; we accept the curse that must follow upon our sins.

This is what the early Christians knew and what we must learn. We have bound ourselves to a covenant, and every covenant implies a law.

Law and liturgy are inseparable. The liturgy exists for the sake of our holiness, our sanctification; and the law exists for the sake of righteousness, to protect and preserve the holiness of the liturgy. All of Catholic morality and every line of canon law exist primarily to protect the sanctity of the sacraments. The law is ordered to the liturgy, not vice versa. The liturgy is primary.

Why does our nation have family law? Maybe we've forgotten. It's because marriage is holy. It is a sacrament, a covenant, an oath sworn in God's name. The law protects the covenant oath. The law preserves the holiness of the sacrament.

Why could I not see all this when I entered the seminary? It was just a few months after my own wedding day that I confessed my boredom with things sacramental. Yet, even then, my best professors were speaking of baptism as a covenant oath. Why could I not see that my wedding vows, too, had all the marks of a biblical covenant?

I could not see it at the time, but I would see it soon—the loveliest of ironies—thanks to the beautiful and fascinating sacrament who walked with me, the one to whom I had pledged my life "as long as we both shall live," the one to whom I said, "Sacraments bore me."

It was by a grace of the sacrament of marriage that God kept me from repeating anything so unsafe.

CHAPTER 7

When Words Are Deeds

THE OATH, WITH its binding power, remains as a sort of religious relic in today's secularist societies. One scholar calls the oath "an ancient ruin still standing." Another refers to it, frankly, as a lingering superstition from the ancient world. The philosopher George Santayana summed it up: "Oaths are fossils of piety."

Indeed, in the United States, where religion has been fairly well purged from the civic life, the state continues to dress its oaths up in the terms and trappings of covenant ritual. Joseph Vining, a renowned legal scholar, points out that the parallels between the practice of law and the practice of religion "are too striking for the lawyer not to see." He goes on to cite many examples: Judges, like priests, wear special vestments; the architecture of the courtroom, like that of a church, is designed "to produce respect, even awe"; in court, the law is cited, like Scripture, as an authoritative text; in court, as in church, etiquette is marked by self-abasement and respect for hierarchy; and, in both places, ritual is paramount.

Oaths, then, have every appearance of being sacred. Yet the skeptical scholars have a point when they say that these trappings are little more than appearances—ancient ruins preserved in their facade, but empty inside. Most Americans, by now, have grown well acclimated to the most strict separation of church and state; and, if they thought about it, they would have to admit that they share the skepticism of the legal scholars.

I write these words less than a decade after an American president was credibly accused of perjury. Do we, as a society, really believe in the power of words to accomplish anything in the material order? I would wager that the most fearsome aspect of oaths, for most of my fellow citizens, is the severe legal penalty for perjury. As for the blessings and curses we invoke when we swear—as for the divine help we call upon—most Americans probably see these as ornamental customs, like the powdered wigs worn by British judges.

But if we have so little regard for oaths, is it any wonder that we have so little understanding of the sacraments?

Utter Mysteries

Modern rationalists don't trust words as much as things and deeds. Words rise for a moment and vanish, like frosty breath on a winter's day. Things matter. Money talks. We speak of "mere words," but "mighty deeds."

It is fair, however, for us to ask if rationalists are consistent in judging words powerless. Or are there occasions when even the most hardened cynic will insist that words accomplish something?

Secular philosophers have pondered the question and have come to a confident "yes." There are times when words are more than "mere words." There are times when words do more than describe. There are times when words are deeds.

This is the contention of "speech–act" theory, which was first proposed by philosopher J. L. Austin in the 1960s and has since become an influential school of thought. Austin pointed out that, while most words are merely descriptive, there are certain phrases that really accomplish what they describe. Once they are uttered, they change things. They can change lives. They can change history. They perform actions. And that's why Austin classified such phrases as "performative utterance."

When a boss says "You're fired," he hasn't merely described a situation. He has caused it to be.

When a woman hears the formula of the wedding vows and responds "I do," she has caused something to be.

Some performative utterances have small stakes: "I bet you five dollars." Others cost many lives: "We declare war."

All of them assume a certain authority ("By the power

vested in me . . ."), and all of them take a certain recogniz-able form ("I hereby dub thee knight").

In the end, these words effect what they signify. They pack power. Perhaps they help us to understand the enduring power of oaths, which most people assume, even if they don't understand.

For example, it is by virtue of the oath of office—not by popular vote or by vote of the electoral college—that a man becomes president of the United States. Lyndon B. Johnson, the thirty-sixth president, described that reality as he relinquished the office to his successor, Richard Nixon: "I think the most pleasant words that . . . ever came into my ears were 'So help me God' that you repeated after that oath. Because at that time, I no longer had the fear that I was the man . . . that would have to carry the terrifying responsibility of protecting the lives of this country and maybe the entire world, unleashing the horrors of some of our great power."

J. L. Austin was not a religious man; nevertheless, he recognized the sacred power of oaths. He said that "swearing puts on record my spiritual assumption of a spiritual shackle."

Maybe oaths and sacraments aren't so unusual as they appear at first glance.

Copy Rites

Still, I can't help but feel a certain degree of sympathy with the modern view. I can remember a time in my own life when I thought that sacraments were holdovers from an age that believed in magic. I saw rituals as mechanical procedures people used to manipulate God.

I came, however, to recognize that those who try to do away with the Church's sacraments inevitably end up replacing them with rituals of their own making. I, for example, felt drawn to extremes in order to deny that baptism held any real power. Many Evangelicals I knew and respected would argue that baptism was merely a public witness to an interior conversion. Following this logic to its inevitable conclusions, they would deny baptism to anyone incapable of having a conversion experience—like infants or small children. But what would we do next? We would establish the "altar call" as a sort of requisite liturgy, an effective sign of newborn faith. And the altar call became for us the practical equivalent of a sacrament. We would have nothing to do with confession, but soon found ourselves ritualizing the personal testimony, or "witness talk." We distrusted the Eucharist, but found ourselves sublimating the matter into what Catholics would call a spiritual communion: "I accept Jesus into my heart as my personal Lord and Savior."

Sacraments resonate with something that is deep within

us, and it is there because God put it there. It is a natural desire, perfected by a supernatural grace. When we don't have sacraments, we feel the need to invent them. In the fourth century, there was an upstart movement to hold the teachings of Christ without the sacraments of Christ. To such heretics, St. Augustine said: "There can be no religious society, whether the religion be true or false, without some sacrament or visible symbol to serve as a bond of union. The importance of these sacraments cannot be overstated, and only scoffers will treat them lightly. For if piety requires them, it must be impiety to neglect them."

Words Louder Than Deeds

The Christian sacraments are unique as "speech acts," because they are acts not of human beings, but of God. Only God has the power to accomplish what the Church claims for the sacraments. Only God's word can completely effect what it signifies. God created matter out of nothing; He has the power to refashion it at will. St. Ambrose put this vividly in a homily preached in the year 391.

> How can something which is bread be the body of Christ? Well, by what words is the consecration effected, and whose words are they? The words of the Lord Jesus. All that is said before are the words of the priest. . . . But when the moment comes for bringing the most holy sacrament into being, the priest does not use his own words any longer: he uses the words of

Christ. Therefore, it is Christ's word that brings this sacrament into being.

What is the word of Christ? It is the word by which all things are made. The Lord commanded and the heavens were made, the Lord commanded and the earth was made, the Lord commanded and the seas were made, the Lord commanded and all creatures came into being.

God's word is living and active. It makes things happen. "He commanded and they were created" (Ps 148:5). And He has shown Himself eager to involve human beings in His work of a new creation, wrought by the sacraments. Here's St. Augustine again: "Everything could well have been done by an angel, but the standing of the human race would have been devalued if God had seemed unwilling to let men act as the agents of His Word to men." And so He did, and so He does.

All the fathers of the Church saw the sacraments in this way—as accomplishing a new creation, by the power of the Word of God. St. Gregory of Nyssa wrote:

The bread is at first common bread. But when the sacramental action consecrates it, it is called the Body of Christ, for it becomes the Body of Christ. . . . So with the sacramental oil; so with the wine. Before the blessing, they are worth little. But afterward they are made holy by the Spirit. The same power of the word makes the priest worthy of veneration and honor. The new blessing separates him from his common life with the people. Yesterday he was one of the crowd. . . . Now, suddenly, he has become a guide, a leader, a teacher of righteousness, an instructor in hidden mysteries. And this he does without any change in body or form. But, while he appears to be the man he was before, his invisible soul has really been transformed to a higher condition by some invisible power and grace.

Performative Arts

It is the word that performs the deed, for it is the divine Word Who utters the word. "Take away the word, and the water is neither more nor less than water," St. Augustine said. "The word is added to the element, and there results the sacrament, as if itself also a kind of visible word."

There is a beautiful symmetry here between the preaching of the early Christians and the insights of modern philosophy.

It is not unusual or unnatural for words to wield power. We may speak of a whole category of human phrases that perform mighty deeds. Among these are oaths and covenants. "An oath highlights the relationship of human speech with God's truth" (CCC, n. 2151).

We should not be surprised that when God utters such phrases, they work with divine power. Furthermore, we should not be surprised that when God chooses to perform wonders among His people, He does so in ways they might recognize, in ways they have always desired, in ways that really work: through sacraments.

CHAPTER 8

❦❦❦

THE ENGINE
OF HISTORY

I F GOD'S WORD in the sacraments is most like His word "in the beginning," then we should spend a moment examining the nature of His word of creation. We read in the Psalms that "He commanded and they were created" (Ps 148:5). But what form did His command take, as we find it expressed in the opening chapters of the Bible?

We read in the Book of Genesis that God created the universe in six days and rested on the seventh. We'll leave aside the acrimonious debates about the literal meaning of these "days," and ask why the inspired author—and the inspiring God—chose to describe creation in this way. Why does God make the cosmos in six days and not in an instant? He is God; He is all-powerful, and all He needed to do was "command" and the world would be created. Moreover, why would He need to "rest" on the seventh day? An omnipotent, spiritual being does not grow tired or suffer any other imperfections.

God accomplished His creation and revealed it to us in

a particular way. He did so, however, not for His own sake, but for ours (see CCC, n. 293). God gained nothing by stretching the effort into six days of narrative time; nor was He refreshed by taking the seventh day off.

The seven days of Genesis are intended to signify something about God, the cosmos, and their relationship. Consider the commentary of Rabbi Samson Raphael Hirsch: "The physically perceptible world was already completed in the first six days. . . . However, real completion came only with the Seventh Day. The seventh day did this not by adding yet another order of perceptible creations to the physical world . . . the seventh day added the Invisible to the perceptible; it established the bond between the Creator and His creation, between the Master and His work, between God and His world."

Rabbi Hirsch, following the ancient sages, maintains that the bond between Creator and creation is a specific kind of bond. We may call it *sacramental,* since, as he says, it unites the Invisible with the perceptible. But, to describe this bond most accurately, we must also call it *covenantal.*

The Great Oath

It is no accident that God "hallowed" the seventh day (Gen 2:2). The Hebrew word for the number seven, *sheva,* evokes a wealth of intended meaning. *Sheva* is the root of the word *saba,* which means "fullness and completion." The earth was full and creation complete on the seventh day. At the other end of the Bible, in the Book of Revelation, we find an abundance of sevens signifying the end of the world—history come to its completion, in the fullness of time (see, for example, Rev 15:1).

But the word *sheva* has a still-closer kinship with another word: *shava*. *Shava* is the verb for swearing a covenant oath. Its literal meaning is "to seven oneself." The verb for swearing a covenant is built upon the number seven. Why is it binding for human beings to "seven" themselves? Because that is what God did at the dawn of creation.

By blessing the seventh day, God swore a covenant to His world. He is not just proprietor of creation. He is not just master to a race of slaves. He is Father to a family. If God had stopped on the sixth day, we would be His creatures, slaves, and private property. But He went on and blessed the seventh day, and took a rest, and invited humankind into that rest. That action represents the covenant relationship that He established with his creation. And what is a covenant? A family bond, a sacred family bond.

The seventh day, then, was the sign of the covenant—the sacrament of the covenant. Its name was used synonymously with the covenant. God commands Israel to observe "the sabbath throughout their generations, as a perpetual covenant. It is a sign forever between Me and the people of Israel that in six days the Lord made heaven and earth, and on the seventh day He rested" (Ex 31:16–17).

God made the universe in six days, and on the seventh

He bound Himself to it forever. The first Book of Enoch, an ancient Jewish text that is quoted in the New Testament (see Jude 14), refers to this action as the "Great Oath" that bound all the wild forces of nature: water, wind, weather, heavenly bodies, and earthly fertility. These the author lists off in a long litany, and in the voice of Enoch, he concludes: "And this oath is mighty over them, and through it their paths are preserved, and their course is not destroyed."

God established order in the cosmos by an oath that is legally binding. He swore His oath in a liturgical action, too, by blessing the sabbath day. Thus, by a single speech act, a single performative utterance, He transformed the cosmos from a mere creation into a family home and a holy temple.

This is the power of His word in the sacraments, because this was the power of His word "in the beginning." It is God's word—with the water, with the bread and wine—that makes our churches into holy temples, that transforms human children into children of God.

Lucky Sevens

Genesis tells the story and forever sets the model for covenant. Ever afterward, it was in imitation of God that men swore covenant oaths by sevening themselves. We find echoes of the divine oath in the seven clean animals sacrificed by Noah aboard the ark. We encounter the notion again when Abraham takes seven ewe lambs in order to swear a covenant of kinship with Abimelech. Afterward, "that place was called Beer-sheva; because there both of them swore an oath" (Gen 21:31). The name "Beer-sheva" means, literally, both "well of the seven" and "well of the oath."

Abraham's grandson Jacob will repeat the pattern of "sevening," when he serves Laban for seven years for the privilege of marrying Leah and then another seven years to enter a marriage covenant with Rachel (Gen 29:20, 27).

Perhaps the most striking example of swearing an oath by means of sevens appears in the Second Book of Chronicles. It's worth quoting at length, as it brings together the sevens, the oath, the covenant, the sacrifice, the sabbath rest, and the liturgical celebration:

> *They sacrificed to the Lord on that day . . . seven hundred oxen and seven thousand sheep. And they entered into a covenant to seek the Lord, the God of their fathers, with all their heart and with all their soul. . . . They took oath to the Lord with a loud voice, and with shouting, and with trumpets, and with horns. And all Judah rejoiced over the oath; for they had sworn with all their heart, and had sought Him with their whole desire, and He was found by them, and the Lord gave them rest round about. . . . And there was no more war until the thirty-fifth year of the reign of Asa. (2 Chr 15:11–19)*

Rabbi Hirsch explained the gravity of swearing in this way:

> *The verb [shava] . . . is obviously derived from seven. . . . [It] would mean nothing else but to subject oneself to "the seventh," or, more fully, to subordinate oneself with all of one's material world to the Invisible Lord and Master, to surrender oneself to Him with all of one's physical existence. . . . It would be literally . . . an act of "taking upon oneself" the Name of God, the placing of one's self beneath the Name of God . . . total submission, under oath, to the authority of the Lord and master Who is invisible but nonetheless is present everywhere . . . a genuine pledge of one's whole physical being to the veracity of one's word.*

One cannot invoke God's name in this way without accepting His fatherly authority over the matter under oath—without accepting all the consequences of the oath for "one's whole physical being." It is little wonder that God warned His people against swearing rashly: "You shall not take the name of the Lord your God in vain; for the Lord will not hold him guiltless who takes His name in vain" (Ex 20:7).

All actions have consequences. Actions undertaken in violation of a covenant can have catastrophic and even cosmic consequences, because they are offenses against the almighty Creator of the world. Old Testament scholar

Margaret Barker speaks of the aftereffects of sins against the covenant of creation: "To break this covenant was to release forces which could destroy Creation. It is interesting that the Hebrew word for covenant, *berith,* is thought to be related to the word for 'binding.' " Sin against the covenant, then, is what unbinds, unleashes the forces of disorder in the world. Rabbi Hirsch puts it in terms that are as stark as those in the Book of Revelation: "Perjury committed by one who swears can bring about the destruction of an entire world"; and he refers us to the fifth chapter of Zechariah, where God curses the household of those who swear oaths falsely.

God swore His covenant in order to complete His creation. Now all creation is subject to the principles of the covenant. Human beings swear oaths and make covenants because God first showed them how. To swear in this way is to imitate God, with the power of God as surety.

Championship Series

Only when we begin to comprehend the importance of covenant oaths can we begin to understand the principles that order the events of history—at least as we encounter sacred history in the Bible. This is true, in the first place, because God has revealed Himself to us through a series of covenants.

In creation, He established a covenant bond with humanity. It was a marital bond under the sign of the Sabbath, since the marriage of Adam and Eve was sealed on the seventh day. The Adamic covenant extends beyond the primal couple, however. It is foundational for all the other covenants, since Adam is the father of the entire human family. Adam's name is not only the name of an individual, the founding father of the human race, but it's also the Hebrew word for humanity—much like Americans use the word "Washington" to denote the founding father of their country and the capital of the country, as well.

The second covenant that God established was with Noah. Whereas God made the first covenant with a married couple, He extended the second to an entire household, an extended family. When God punished humanity with a devastating flood, he pledged to keep Noah and his kin safe throughout the flood. As the waters receded, He set His rainbow in the sky as a covenant sign, and He pledged never again to wipe out the human family by flood.

The third covenant was with the patriarch Abraham, who was chieftain over an entire tribe that God wished to identify as His own. The tribe included not only Abraham and his wife, but also Abraham's relatives and all their household servants, who probably numbered in the hundreds or thousands. God promised Abraham a vast land where his natural descendants might be blessed as a nation, and then a kingdom, until eventually all the families of the earth would be blessed through him and his seed. The sign of the covenant was circumcision. Abraham had a son Isaac, and Isaac had a son named Jacob, and Jacob had twelve sons, all of whom fathered large families that became the twelve tribes of Israel (after the new name God gave to Jacob).

At Mount Sinai God established a fourth covenant, now with Moses as the representative of all Israel. The Lord directed Moses to lead the twelve tribes out of slavery in Egypt and to ratify a covenant that made them a holy nation. The sign of this covenant was the Passover, the sacrificial meal that transformed the twelve tribes into God's national family, Israel. God gave the Ten Commandments and other statutes to Moses so that Israel would have its own national constitution; He called the tribes to occupy the Promised Land of Canaan as their inheritance. Yet Israel sinned by worshipping the golden calf, and by their sin, the Israelites merited death. They were saved only because Moses invoked the oath God swore to bless Abraham and his descendants forever. The oath God swore in Genesis 22 turned out to be Israel's salvation in Exodus 32.

God made the fifth and last of the major Old Testament covenants with King David. God covenanted with David to build a worldwide kingdom, whose sign would be the everlasting throne of David's son (see Ps 89:3–4 and Ps 110:4). Now the covenant extended its reach from the nation of Israel to a newly established kingdom, whose monarch was destined to rule over all the nations. David and his son, Solomon, carried out God's plan by incorporating many of the surrounding nations and city-states into the covenant. Since kings take tribute from subject nations, this also meant that foreigners would make annual visits to Jerusalem, where they would hear God's law and learn his fatherly wisdom from Solomon. As a result, the gentiles learned to worship the one true God, while God prepared them to be eventually restored to His family, with the coming of the real Son of David, Jesus Christ.

There we have the Old Testament covenants in sequence leading up to the coming of Christ: first with Adam, second with Noah, third with Abraham, fourth with Moses, and fifth with David. Note that each covenant extended God's reach to an ever-larger family: first to a couple, then to a household, then to a tribe, then to a nation, and finally to all the nations.

But it is only with Jesus Christ that all the covenants found their definitive fulfillment. Jesus bore all the curses of the previously broken covenants, so that He could ratify the New Covenant in the self-offering of His flesh and blood. This New Covenant permanently binds together both Jews and gentiles in one universal divine family: the one, holy, catholic, and apostolic Church.

In the pages of Scripture, we see how covenants affect the broad sweep of history. But that is possible only because they affect the small details, as well. The history of the world is a chronicle of blessings and curses, and many of those that appear in the biblical narrative, appear as consequences of the sworn oaths of God's people.

Sevens Up

It was God's Great Oath that set creation in motion. Is it any wonder that subsequent human oaths have proved to be turning points in human history? Indeed, the biblical authors show a profound awareness of the power of human oaths, and throughout the Bible oaths serve as catalysts for events and as an effective literary device to advance the plot.

Search the Scriptures, from cover to cover, and you'll find many examples of people swearing oaths, making covenants. In most cases, the texts relate these episodes casually and without elaboration. So we must assume that the narrators expected their readers to have an appreciation for oaths, their power, and their place in society. We have already mentioned Genesis 21, in which Abraham and Abimelech swear an oath and make a covenant. The narrative makes it clear that the oath is what sealed the covenant: "Both of them swore an oath. So they made a covenant . . ." (vv. 31–32). The epic of Abraham's family moves forward because of another oath, this one sworn by the senior servant of the patriarch's household, who promises to find a suitable wife for Isaac (Gen 24:3, 8–9). He fulfills the oath, of course, thereby ensuring that Abraham's line of descent will continue. Consider another example, from several centuries later, when the Israelites were beginning their conquest of the promised land (Jos 9). One of the native tribes, the Gibeonites, disguised themselves as foreigners on a long journey from a distant land—carrying moldy bread and worn-out sacks and wineskins. They hoodwinked Joshua into guaranteeing them peace and the freedom to live on their lands. The leaders of Israel swore an oath and made a covenant with them (Jos 9:15). And, in spite of the Gibeonites' deception, God honored the covenant. More centuries passed, and Saul, the king of the Israelites, led a campaign of ethnic cleansing against the Gibeonites, putting many to death (2 Sam 21). For personal and political gains, Saul violated the treaty of his forefathers and brought upon Israel the curses of the covenant. Soon famine descended on the lands, and the covenant curse was lifted only after Saul died and seven of his sons were handed over to be hanged by the Gibeonites.

King Saul, perhaps, did not consider oaths as truly binding over the course of generations. Or maybe he disbelieved that oaths held any real power at all. His life, in fact, was marked by rash oaths. Once, in the heat of battle, he swore, "Cursed be the man who eats food until it is evening and I am avenged on my enemies" (1 Sam 14:24). His son Jonathan, unaware of the oath, arrived at the camp and helped himself to a taste of honey. Immediately bystanders informed him of the violation, and he himself saw the consequences: "My father has troubled the land" (v. 29). As a result of his father's oath, Jonathan soon faced a sentence of death. The people spared him, however, swearing in their turn, "As the Lord lives, there shall not one hair of his head fall to the ground" (14:45).

Saul and all his offspring perished. Yet his dynasty found succession because Jonathan had sworn a "sacred covenant" with David (1 Sam 18:3, 20:8). The two friends had exchanged clothing as an outward sign of their covenant-family bond. David donned the robes of a prince, and Jonathan took on the armor of a soldier. "And Jonathan made David swear again by his love for him; for he loved him as he loved his own soul" (1 Sam 20:17). Thus, by their covenant, they were brothers, more truly than if they had been born of the same parents. In time, however, Saul would come to envy and fear David's popularity, and he would declare David his mortal enemy. When Saul's line ended with defeat in battle, all his oaths would find ironic fulfillment as David, the "brother" of his son, assumed the throne.

David stands in contrast to Saul, if we consider the way the two men used oaths. David began his reign by honoring his covenant with Jonathan; he adopted Jonathan's handicapped son, Mephibosheth, and fed him every day at the royal table. Furthermore, God protected David by keeping him from swearing oaths he would violate. When David's firstborn son, Absalom, rebelled, David assured Absalom's mother: "As the Lord lives, not one hair of your son shall fall to the ground" (2 Sam 14:11). Of course, the fulfillment of this oath was not in David's power. Indeed, Absalom met his death when he was riding and his head became caught in the branches of an oak. Absalom died "hanging between heaven and earth" (2 Sam 18:9), without a hair of his head falling to the ground; but David's word in his oath was preserved.

At the end of his life, David ceded succession not to his firstborn son, but to his son Solomon, because of an oath invoked by Solomon's mother, Bathsheba (whose name means "Daughter of the Oath").

No Change for a Seven

The oath is the tide that sweeps history along. Everything in the Bible hangs on this truth—tribal relations, dynastic succession, and the rise and fall of households and temples, marriages and nations. Everything in the experience of God's people, and everything in the lives of individuals—everything at all revolves around the oaths the people swore and how faithfully those oaths were fulfilled.

We must learn never to think of the oath as a mere literary motif or an ornament of ancient epics. No, a sworn oath invests human language with divine power.

When the first Christians pondered their salvation, they read the Old Testament and founded their hope on the ancient oaths. For, in all disputes, "an oath is final for confirmation. . . . So when God desired to show more convincingly to the heirs of the promise the unchangeable character of His purpose, He interposed with an oath, so that . . . we who have fled for refuge might have strong encouragement to seize the hope set before us" (Heb 6:16, 18).

From the first "fiat" of Genesis to the last trumpets of Revelation, history unfolds according to the law of the covenant, the blessings and curses of our oaths. What are the oaths we swear today? The same passage from Hebrews, just quoted, distinguishes between "elementary doctrine" and the doctrines of Christian "maturity" (6:1)—and what were these latter but the sacraments, the mysteries kept hidden from the catechumens until their initiation? The author of Hebrews alludes to "ablutions" and "enlightenment" (baptism); "the laying on of hands" (ordination); "repentance" (confession); having "tasted of the heavenly gift" and "tasted of the goodness of the Word of God" (Eucharist); and the day when Christians "become partakers of the Holy Spirit" (confirmation).

The first generation of Christians understood. Like their Hebrew ancestors, they were bound by oaths, and those oaths were demanding. Each came complete with a binding law. But these oaths were the only "sure and steadfast anchor of the soul"; the sacraments were the only path "that enters into the inner shrine behind the curtain, where Jesus has gone as a forerunner on our behalf" (Heb 6:19–20). For the sacraments were outward signs that united "the Invisible to the perceptible."

How fitting that there are *seven* sacraments by which Christians make and renew their covenant with God. In Christ, the Creator has brought about a "new creation" (see 2 Cor 5:17) by means of the sacraments. He has sevened Himself in a way that altogether surpasses what He did in the beginning.

This is the biblical worldview. It is a sacramental worldview. More than a century ago, Rabbi Hirsch looked at the seven-day Jewish festival of Passover and concluded: "the number seven [is] also meant to make certain that our celebration will indeed serve to elevate all our physical being to God, so that, in and through our festival, God will enter into a sacred covenant with us."

How much more should we say the same—we who mark our lives with the sevenfold rites of the New Covenant!

CHAPTER 9

❧❧❧

TRUST AND
TREACHERY

Oaths create worlds. Oaths form societies. An oath takes people who are disunited, and it binds them together as one.

Human society is untenable and unimaginable without oaths. That is why, in our day and age, even secularist governments invest their oaths with sacred ceremony and divine oversight.

How necessary are oaths? Compare four testimonies from world literature, spread out across two millennia.

The Greek historian Xenophon, writing in the fifth century before Christ, observed: "In every city of Greece there is a law which requires that all citizens shall promise under oath to be unanimous and act in concord, and they take this oath everywhere. The object of this, I think, is that . . . they may obey the laws." The laws of Athens set forth the obligation and the consequences: "All the Athenians shall take this oath over a sacrifice without blemish, as the law enjoins. . . . And they shall pray that he who observes this oath may be blessed abundantly; but that he who does not observe it may perish from the earth, both he and his house."

In North Africa, A.D. 398, St. Augustine wrote that peace between nations was impossible without treaties that were bound by oaths. "Peace is secured by the oaths of barbarians, not only for a single boundary but for whole provinces." The barbarians may have been pagans, but still they honored their oath and feared its curses. Without such oaths, Augustine said, "I do not know whether we can find anywhere on earth to live."

More than a thousand years later, in seventeenth-century England, we find the same message in the writings of Thomas Egerton, Lord Chancellor to King James I. "The law and civil polity of England being chiefly founded upon religion and the fear of God doth use the religious ceremony of an oath not merely in legal proceedings but in other transactions and affairs of importance, esteeming oaths not only the best touchstones of trust in matters of controversy but the safest knot of civil society and the firmest bond to tie all men to the performance of their several duties."

In American history, the best testimony comes from none other than George Washington, the "father of our country." In his famous Farewell Address of 1796, he said: "Let it simply be asked: Where is the security for property, for reputation, for life, if the sense of religious obligation desert the oaths which are the instruments of investigation in courts of justice? And let us with caution indulge the supposition that morality can be maintained without reli-

gion. Whatever may be conceded to the influence of refined education on minds of peculiar structure, reason and
experience both forbid us to expect that national morality
can prevail in exclusion of religious principle."

A Matter of Trust

Oaths create worlds. Oaths form societies. And oaths are
necessarily religious. Without oaths that are guaranteed by
God and respected by citizens, human society falls apart.

And that is just as true for the human society of the
chosen people, the people of God, the Church. We need
oaths, and that is why we have sacraments. Civil oaths—
even in their current weakened form—can teach us why
our sacraments, our covenant oaths are necessary.

Consider, for example, which citizens we require to
take an oath: judges, presidents, members of Congress, soldiers, and witnesses in the courtroom. Until very recently,
all medical doctors had to swear the Hippocratic Oath,
named after the ancient Greek physician Hippocrates.

What do all these people have in common? We cannot
trust them—but we *have* to trust them. Remember the old
saying: "Power tends to corrupt; absolute power corrupts
absolutely." We cannot trust people enough to give them
power over us; yet society cannot keep order—or even exist—unless it entrusts some people with power.

Judges, soldiers, politicians, doctors—they all hold
power over the lives and livelihood of other people. They
all must face constant temptations to abuse that power—

temptations that are too much for anyone to bear. Their job demands that they look to the interests of others even before their own self-interest, and that's asking them to ignore basic human instinct.

Courtroom witnesses hold such power, and they face such temptations. Their testimony will determine the guilt or innocence, the freedom or imprisonment, of a fellow citizen. The court needs that testimony, and so it entrusts witnesses with power. But what if a witness sees some personal benefit in lying? What if he fears that the truth will cost him something—maybe even his life, because of retribution? Or what if the witness himself is actually the guilty party and has so far avoided discovery? The temptation is just too great. Only an oath with divine sanctions can serve to counter such overwhelming worldly interests.

Soldiers, too, must swear an oath. Like witnesses, they must be motivated by something greater than the fear of earthly danger. For one day, they might find themselves on a battlefield with bullets whizzing overhead. Suppose one soldier looks around and sees an escape route that would enable him to desert his comrades in arms. Who wouldn't rather run and live to fight another day? Instinct and common sense tell the soldier to flee for his life. But he must not. He must place the good of his country and his military unit ahead of his own survival. Thus, those who desert under fire are to be shot on sight, by their own comrades; after all, if they get away, who wouldn't want to follow? Military service requires a degree of trust that the soldiers themselves cannot live up to. Yet they *must* live up to it.

So we place them under oath, just as we place witnesses under oath.

Right Hand Up to God

The human condition places us in a difficult spot. We know we need doctors, soldiers, leaders, and civil servants, but we also know human weakness and susceptibility to temptation. We can't trust people to do those jobs. What, then, can we do? We place people under oath, because even though they cannot do the job on their own, perhaps they can do it with God's assistance. That is why many oaths end with the words "So help me, God." That is why, when George Washington took the oath of office, he placed his hand on a Bible opened to Psalm 121:1: "I raise my eyes toward the hills. Whence shall my help come."

God's name provides the surety required for society's trust. For God always gives people the power, the help, and the blessing they need to fulfill their duties, *if* they do not take His name in vain. If, however, they violate their oath, they must face the warning of the Ten Commandments: "The Lord will not hold him guiltless who takes His Name in vain" (Ex 20:7). If they sin, they must bear the corresponding curse.

Again, these principles are implied even in secular oaths. Courtroom oaths and oaths of office, for example, follow an elaborate code of gestures and symbols, and they all come to us from ancient tradition. The swearer puts his left hand on the Bible and raises his right hand upward.

Those gestures, together, constitute an appeal to God. The raised right hand calls upon God in heaven as a witness. It is as if the swearer were saying: "If I am false and no one on earth finds out, still, God will know that I am lying, because God knows everything." The left hand on the Bible, for its part, represents the swearer's acceptance of all the divine punishments recorded in the sacred book.

Of course, there is a flip side to oath-swearing. If the person *does* fulfill the oath, but finds himself disbelieved and dishonored by his human judges, God, Who knows everything, will believe and honor him. And God will vindicate him according to the blessings promised in the Bible to those who live the truth and speak it, as well.

In the Name of God

God's name makes all the difference. His name makes trust possible in human society. Because the swearer invokes God's name, the oath becomes both a pledge and a plea for divine help. Society can count on the individual's pledge; but, far more, society can count on God's active presence and assistance.

Why does the mere mention of God's name make an oath trustworthy? Consider an analogy. Suppose I took out my checkbook right now and wrote you a check for a billion dollars, signing my name with a flourish at the bottom. You'd probably be skeptical. *He's a college professor,* you'd think to yourself. *Where would he get a billion dollars?* You might not even bother to try cashing the check.

But suppose you took a second look, and you noticed that, underneath my signature, was that of a cosigner named Bill Gates, president of Microsoft Corporation and currently the richest man in the world. What would you do, then, with that check in hand? I'll wager that you'd guard it with your life, and you'd make sure to cash it tomorrow morning, if not sooner. Why? Because if Bill Gates's name were invoked underneath my own, the check would become trustworthy.

When we swear an oath, *God* becomes the cosigner. He becomes the surety, the guarantor. God's name becomes attached to our performance. His reputation is on the line. He has to act to vindicate His holy name.

Grace Is the Word

What does all this have to do with sacraments?

Here's the hard truth: We cannot be trusted. Without divine help, we cannot live even part of a single day as we should. We need God's assistance. We need His grace. So we need to be placed under oath, for the sake of our pledged obedience and His promise of help.

Think about humanity's track record. Again and again, God extended His covenants, but His mediators consistently failed to keep them. God gave Adam dominion over the earth; but Adam, fearing for his earthly life, sinned by disobeying God. God saved Noah from the devastating flood; but Noah got drunk and shamed himself. God promised Abraham countless descendants, but still the man gave in to temptation and slept with an Egyptian mistress. God worked great wonders through Moses; yet Moses still doubted, and he offended God so grievously that he was not permitted to enter the Promised Land. God gave David a kingdom, and David showed his gratitude by committing adultery and murder.

We can read salvation history as humanity's consistent failure to keep the covenant. These biblical failures should make us tremble. Moses was the meekest man on earth. Noah was righteous. Abraham was a just man. David was a man after God's own heart. Yet they all failed.

The Old Testament reads like a dismal record of human weakness and failure. Even the best of intentions could not make our ancestors trustworthy men and women.

But then the Word became flesh! God became a man, in Jesus Christ, so that He Himself could take up the covenant oath for us. Christ assumed human nature with all its debts, obligations, and weaknesses. Then He perfected that human nature in Himself, with His divine life and power as He lived it out—as an infant, as a child, as a preadolescent, as a teenager, as a young adult, and as a mature adult. As a son and as a man, He perfected all human life and all human relations. Finally, He established a *New Covenant* by becoming a cosigner to the Old Covenant. He accepted the burden of the Old Covenant curse upon Himself. In so doing, He instituted in His own body and blood the sacrament by which the New Covenant is constituted.

Christianity is the only religion in all the world and in all of history in which God swears an oath on the part of mankind. Christ himself is the one, true dependable sacrament. His life thus became the source of all of our sacraments.

Fidelity Savings

When we receive the sacraments, we enter into the oath. And the sacraments, like any oath, change the nature of our subsequent actions. Ever afterward, our hours are richer, charged with grace, but more demanding, as well. The stakes are higher.

When we receive the sacraments, we invite God to take an active part in the events of our everyday life. We are leaning on Him as our trust. We know He will vindicate His name—and ours, if only we are faithful.

The sacraments do not guarantee *our* fidelity; for we remain free agents, able to choose good or evil. But they do guarantee God's powerful assistance and abiding presence to help us choose rightly. Moreover, they establish, renew, and strengthen our family bond with God; and they qualify us for His covenant blessings, even as they subject us to His judgment.

If we understand these consequences—and if we believe in God's knowledge, power, and providential care—then we can begin to understand what our ancestors believed about oaths and sacraments. Oaths provided the only sure stability in a society shared by sinful, weak, and ever-changing people. And God's Church is surely such a society.

If human society secured peace by means of oaths sworn before God, how much more should we find peace in an oath sworn by God Himself?

CHAPTER 10

❦❧

To Tell
the Truth

OATHS PROMISED GREAT benefits to those who kept them—world peace, family membership, a military career—but the consequences of infidelity were so dire that most people hesitated to swear at all. Indeed, in many places, people would not use the special language of swearing in common speech, for fear of inadvertently triggering the curses, as King Saul had done. In the sixteenth century, the novelist Miguel de Cervantes, author of *Don Quixote,* avoided placing oaths even on the lips of his fictional characters. Instead, he interrupted the novel's dialogue and provided a description: "and here he rapped out a round oath." By substituting a descriptive phrase, Cervantes kept himself and his readers from the speech act of swearing, with all its possible effects.

A few people, however, went even further than this. They went so far as to deny that oaths had any place at all in a Christian's life or in Christian society. Moreover, they cited Jesus Himself as their authority:

Again you have heard that it was said to the men of old, "You shall not swear falsely, but shall perform to the Lord what you have sworn." But I say to you, Do not swear at all, either by heaven, for it is the throne of God, or by the earth, for it is his footstool, or by Jerusalem, for it is the city of the great King. And do not swear by your head, for you cannot make one hair white or black. Let what you say be simply "Yes" or "No"; anything more than this comes from evil. (Mt 5:33–37)

The case against oaths seems even more compelling when we hear Jesus' words echoed in the Letter of St. James: "But above all, my brethren, do not swear, either by heaven or by earth or with any other oath, but let your yes be yes and your no be no, that you may not fall under condemnation" (Jas 5:12). These words seem to be an absolute prohibition, and an important one at that. The "above all" sounds ominous if we consider the prominent role that oaths play in a wide range of activities of modern society, from Boy Scout meetings to murder trials.

This is especially important to us as we consider Christian sacraments as sacred oaths of the New Covenant. Could Jesus—who seems to have prohibited oaths—really have intended us to take and renew these particular oaths until the end of time?

Swear Words and Curses

Jesus spoke against oaths in the Sermon on the Mount. In commenting on the passage, St. Augustine said: "It seems to me that this was said, not because it is a sin to swear truly, but because it is a heinous sin to swear falsely, and so He warned us not to swear at all because He wished to keep us far from that sin."

The Christian tradition has never understood our Lord's words to indicate a sweeping prohibition. Jesus Himself used oaths in His speech. Indeed, Jesus is the only person in the gospels to utter the word "amen," which was an ancient oath form. (Often in New Testament translations, the Hebrew word "amen" is rendered in English as "truly" or "verily.") In John's gospel alone, Jesus uses the double amen—the most solemn form—a total of twenty-five times, usually punctuating our Lord's most important statements. For example, most of Jesus' teachings on the sacraments are presented with the assurance of His oath: "Truly, truly *[Amen, amen]*, I say to you, unless one is born of water and the Spirit, he cannot enter the kingdom of God" (Jn 3:5). "Truly, truly *[Amen, amen]*, I say to you, unless you eat the flesh of the Son of man and drink His blood, you have no life in you" (Jn 6:53).

Following after Jesus, every Christian society has honored oaths. St. Paul himself, in the very pages of Scripture, swears by God at least twice (see 2 Cor 1:23 and Gal 1:20).

What, then, was Jesus talking about when He forbade swearing?

Jesus warned against rash and private oaths: that is, the misuse of oath swearing. The swearing of oaths had a specific purpose in God's law of the Old Covenant, and that purpose was public, official, and juridical. Oath swearing, like the infliction of "eye for eye, tooth for tooth" punishment, was intended to take place only in the context of a properly constituted authority. And so, just as private citizens were never expected to privately try a thieving neighbor in the living room and imprison him in the hall closet, private citizens were never expected to invoke the name of God lightly in an oath or to privately usurp this essentially public act reserved to proper authorities.

Swearing oaths without proper authority, like imprisoning neighbors without proper authority, implies an enormous arrogance. For the true purpose of oaths is to solemnly invoke the aid of God when a person is called upon to perform some sacred task for the common good—a task that they are not, in fact, capable of doing by their own strength. One of the central meanings of such public, official, and juridical oaths in the Old Testament was to openly declare a real dependence on God's help.

It seems that, in Jesus' day, people commonly misused the language of swearing. Since this is common in our own day, also, we might have special insight into the problem. How often, in ordinary conversation, do we hear phrases like "by God," "God damn it," "swear to God," "God is my witness," "strike me dead," "for heaven's sake," "for

Christ's sake," "What in God's name . . . ?"—or, one of my personal favorites: "Cross my heart and hope to die, stick a needle in my eye." All these have one thing in common: They are traditional oath forms. By design, they are un-suited to use in everyday speech. People should use them only after deliberation, only in prayer, and only in ways that are approved by God.

In the days when Jesus and James lived in Jerusalem, people often misused oaths. Sometimes they would try to evade the appearance of sin by swearing by God's Temple instead of by God, or by the Temple's gold instead of by the Temple (see Mt 23:16–22). But Jesus wanted to put an end to this immoral, insincere, and irreverent speech. So He abolished not oath swearing, but the misuse of oaths.

Oaths are a sign of covenant, and covenant establishes sacred kinship, not a business contract or a magic spell. Oaths are to be invoked not by private individuals calling on God like a lapdog, but in the context of covenant rela-tionship with God—particularly when that covenant de-mands of us more than we have.

On-the-Job Training

It is significant that the Letter of James cites Job in this context. In Job 31, Job swears his famous "oath of inno-cence," a prayer in a strictly juridical form that pleads in-nocence and invokes the justice of God if Job has done any wrong. It begins with an appeal to God's justice in Job

31:3–4: "Does not calamity befall the unrighteous, and disaster the workers of iniquity? Does not He see my ways, and number all my steps?" Then the oath continues with a litany of conditional curses in the form of "if I did *X,* then let God visit *Y* on me in His justice."

Job's oath, far from being defiant, is a reverent oath, arising from desperation. Job calls on God to bear witness to his innocence; He trusts that God will do so. It is only after Job recites this oath that God breaks His silence. God answers Job by vindicating his innocence and restoring his fortunes twofold (see Job 42:7–10). James refers us to Job's example to show us that the proper use of oath swearing is a prayer.

In oaths, we call upon God's Holy Name for help in a situation that is beyond our strength. It makes perfect sense, then, that James established the *proper* use of oaths in the verses immediately following verse 12. He asks, "Is anyone sick?"—that is: Do any members of the community suffer more than they can bear? If so, James refers them to a *sacramentum* of the early Church that is still practiced today: the sacrament of anointing of the sick. Anointing, like all sacraments, is an oath by which we call upon God's Name and by which God renews His grace of sacred kinship with us through the covenant of Christ.

Like Jesus, James warned his congregation against the practice of making statements and then guaranteeing them by rashly appealing to God as a witness. He did this, as Augustine said, "not because it is a sin to swear truly, but because it is a heinous sin to swear falsely." Still, he provided the proper context for the sacramental oaths of the New Covenant. He did this, moreover, in traditional scriptural terms, using the example of a great saint of the Old Testament.

More on Oaths

The bottom line, for Jesus, for James, and for all Christians, is this: When God's name is used in an oath, He becomes an active partner in the transaction. As Christians, we are already covenant partners with God; by baptism and the Eucharist, we have already placed ourselves under oath. Baptism is a kind of oath of office, because it unites us to Christ's threefold office of priest, prophet, and king. Therefore, we should demonstrate complete integrity in speech, letting our "yes" mean "yes" and our "no" mean "no." While there is a place for oaths in society, our word should in most cases be enough.

After all, people who swear and curse habitually usually do so in order to give their words more force than they really deserve, or to bolster their sagging credibility. For a practicing Christian, this should not be necessary.

If we want to recover the ancient Church's sense of the sacredness of the sacraments, we must also recover the first Christians' reverence for oaths—and the corresponding respect for plain, honest speech. Our everyday conversation is, in a sense, an outward sign of our constant fidelity to the covenant oath we have sworn with God.

The *Catechism of the Catholic Church* points out the practical ways we can live this constancy from day to day.

- We must never use the language of oaths to make a false statement (nn. 2150–2152).
- Even legitimate secular oaths may be refused by Christians who are prepared to accept the consequences of that refusal (n. 2155).
- We should exercise discretion in invoking God as witness to our speech. This does not mean that we shut Him out of our everyday life. Rather, "Discretion in calling upon God is allied with a respectful awareness of His presence, which all of our assertions either witness to or mock" (n. 2153).
- We should not swear oaths administered by people who have no right to do so. In the civil order, this rules out membership in secret societies, such as Masonic lodges, for example. In the sacramental order, it forbids our taking sacraments outside the Catholic Church (n. 2155).
- We must never bind ourselves by oath to do something evil. An oath that requires us to sin is itself sinful and must be refused (n. 2155).
- We should never use what are colloquially called "swear words" and "curses." We should handle God's name with care and affection.

As Creator and Lord, God is the norm of all truth. Jesus said, "I am . . . the truth" (Jn 14:6). Human speech is either in accord with truth Himself or in opposition to Him. A truthful, legitimate oath highlights the correspondence of human speech with God's truth. A false oath calls on God to be witness to a lie. Lies under oath are the essence of infidelity, unfaithfulness. They are acts of contempt toward God.

The great martyr St. Thomas More suffered death because he would not swear falsely. In the play based on his life, *A Man for All Seasons,* More pleads with his daughter not to take oaths lightly: "When a man takes an oath, Meg, he's holding his own self in his own hands. Like water. And if he opens his fingers then—he needn't hope to find himself again."

CHAPTER 11

❧✶❧

SUNDAY SWEARING

THE NOTIONS OF oath and covenant are as foreign to modern cultures as they were foundational to ancient cultures. We have lost something that our ancestors could not live without. What we need to learn is that we cannot live without them either—not, at least, if we want to live as Christians.

When the prophets prepared Israel for Jesus, they spoke of His work as the "new covenant" and the "everlasting covenant." When, at last, Jesus came, He spoke of His saving work in the same terms: "the covenant in my blood" and the "new covenant." His apostles, in their turn, used the very same phrases as they preached the Gospel and wrote their letters to distant congregations. Thus, the salvation we know in Jesus Christ is *nothing at all* if it is not covenantal.

For what is our salvation? Some people say it is salvation from sin, and that is true, as far as it goes. But it does not go far enough. For we are not merely saved *from* sin; we are saved *for* sonship. We are children of God. As

Christians, this is our primary identity (see 1 Jn 3:1–2), and this is the primary reason why God became man: so that we might become "sons in the Son," to borrow the famous phrase of St. Athanasius. God stooped down to become man in order to raise us up as His children, to become "partakers of the divine nature" (2 Pet 1:4). The Son of God became a Son of Man so that the children of men might become children of God. Baptized into Christ, we enter the life of the Trinity, the eternal family of God! Salvation could not get any better than this.

Don't get me wrong: The forgiveness of sins is a wonderful thing; but to be a child of God is so much more. The early Christians dared to call our salvation "divinization" and "deification." We are made divine! St. Basil the Great put it boldly, in A.D. 375, when he enumerated the gifts of the Spirit: "abiding in God, being made like God— and, highest of all, being made God."

The grace we receive in the sacraments is the essence of our divinization. Grace is our sharing in the life of God, as children share in the life of their father. This "adoption" is God's gift to us, given freely. And He gives it to us by means of His covenant, which is sealed and renewed through sacramental signs.

Remember: In the biblical world, covenant was the normal way of making a family bond. Without a valid covenant, there could be no true familial relationship. Thus, it is only through the new and everlasting covenant that we can enter into the family of God.

Mass Destruction

The covenant and the oath: These terms are so closely related that the Bible sometimes uses them synonymously, as when Zechariah speaks of God's "holy covenant, the oath which He swore" (Lk 1:72). And so the covenant is the oath; and the oath is the covenant.

A covenant oath need not be sworn by words; sometimes it was wordlessly enacted by a ritual sign, such as animal sacrifice, circumcision, or a common meal. These signs, too, were so closely associated with the covenant as to be synonymous with it. Sometimes, for example, we read of "the covenant of circumcision" (Acts 7:8) and sometimes simply "the circumcision" (Col 4:11). And so the cut *is* the covenant. Jesus Himself equated the sign of His covenant with the covenant that it sealed: "This cup . . . is the new covenant in My blood" (Lk 22:20). And so the cup *is* the covenant.

In the sacraments—especially the Mass—the first Christians enacted their oath, and so they renewed their family bond. The famous modern biblical scholar George Mendenhall is insistent on this point. An expert on ancient covenants, Mendenhall demonstrates conclusively that the early Church observed the Eucharist—or, better, *swore* the Eucharist—as its covenant oath. Among his many reasons are the following:

1. "[O]aths . . . sometimes took the form of nonver-

bal gestures," and one of the most common oath signs, in Israel and elsewhere, was a meal of bread and wine. The Eucharist, then, provided a covenant ritual familiar to many Semitic peoples, at least in its appearances.

2. Most covenants assumed a "ritual identification of persons with the sacrifice" that they offered. Think, for example, of Abraham with the slaughtered beasts. The implication is a self-identification and self-curse: "May this happen to me if I am unfaithful." In the Eucharist, the identification of priest and offering is complete. Jesus declares the bread and wine to be truly His body and blood. That identification extends, further, to those who are "in Christ"—that is, the Christians who receive the sacrament. In the words of St. Paul: "We who are many are one body, for we all partake of the one bread" (1 Cor 10:17). This identity comes from our oneness with the Lord: "The cup of blessing which we bless, is it not a communion in the blood of Christ? The bread which we break, is it not a communion in the body of Christ?" (1 Cor 10:16). Mendenhall comments: "By eating and drinking, early Christians were identifying themselves with the person of Jesus, taking Jesus' body and blood into their own bodies."

3. Jesus commanded His apostles to "Do this in re-membrance of Me" (1 Cor 11:24), and "remembrance" was a common ancient form of oath. In 2 Samuel 14:11ff, we find an elderly woman asking King David to "remember his God." David responds by immediately swearing an oath ("As Yahweh lives . . ."). To remember

one's God, then, was to enact an oath. To break bread "in remembrance" of the God-Man is to swear the oath of the Christians.

4. Pliny the Younger knew this. Mendenhall cites Pliny's interpretation of Christian worship as *sacramentum* (see chapter 5). Pliny offers no text as evidence because "the actual substance of the oath is expressed not in words but in the act itself: the early Christians were swearing to *embody* Christ." The Eucharist was reason enough for Pliny to punish a Christian for sedition, since it was a wordless, enacted oath, sworn in the name of a divinity other than the Roman emperor.

5. Finally, Mendenhall notes that every oath called down curses, which could be enforced only by acts of God; and the first Christians certainly believed this to be true of the Eucharist. St. Paul warned the Corinthians that "anyone who eats and drinks without discerning the body, eats and drinks judgment upon himself. That is why many of you are weak and ill, and some have died" (1 Cor 11:29–30). Sickness and death are classic examples of the divine punishments invoked in the self-imprecations of ancient covenants. Those who did not fulfill their promises could expect God to visit them with severe judgments that they themselves had invited. Paul's teaching is inexplicable apart from the beliefs and practices surrounding covenant oaths in the ancient world.

The Eucharist, then as now, had all the marks of a covenant oath. It is a formal act, an outward sign, that renews a close family relation. It includes a pledge to embody Christ, confirmed by the traditional word "amen." It includes the customary sentence of life or death, blessing or curse, upon fulfillment or nonfulfillment.

The Mass Makes History

Much seems foreign to us when we confront the Bible's understanding of the sacraments. We are unaccustomed to the close association of law and liturgy. We are unfamiliar with a culture dominated by the swearing of oaths. And some people are downright offended or embarrassed when they read of curses, divine wrath, and punishment. There are even theologians who want to dismiss these as the residue of primitive religion—the bad old days when people worshipped nasty, vengeful, and unenlightened gods.

Yet there it remains, in the midst of a profound theological meditation on the Eucharist, by St. Paul, the most sophisticated theologian in the apostolic Church. It is there, too, in Jesus' own teachings on hell and judgment. In fact, the New Testament concludes with a visionary text that portrays the judgment of the world in terms that are almost exclusively liturgical.

The Book of Revelation, like the Letter to the Hebrews, shows the deep communion between the Church's sacramental worship on earth and the angels' spiritual worship in the courts of heaven. We should note that even angels pray by swearing oaths (see Rev 10:5–6). This common worship makes for powerful prayer before the throne of God. Indeed, this heavenly-earthly worship appears as the driving force in the history of the world. History unfolds, in Revelation, as a series of covenant blessings and curses. John portrays earthly destruction in terms of a terrible Passover. Seven angels pour out the seven chalices of God's wrath, which issue in seven plagues. The emptying of the chalices is a liturgical action, a libation of wine poured upon the land. (Indeed, both sevens and liturgical images abound in Revelation: There are seven golden lampstands, seven spirits, seven stars, seven churches, seven seals, seven trumpets, and seven chalices—to name just seven.)

In light of the Passover's fulfillment in the Eucharist, this imagery becomes all the more striking. Chapters 15 to 17 of Revelation show us the seven plagues within a liturgical setting: The angels appear with harps, vested as priests in the heavenly Temple; they sing the song of Moses and the song of the Lamb (ch. 15). This liturgy means death to God's enemies, but salvation to His Church. Thus, the angels cry: "For men have shed the blood of saints and prophets, and You have given them blood to drink. It is their due!" (Rev 16:6).

Passover, the Eucharist, and the heavenly liturgy, then, are two-edged swords. While the chalices of the covenant bring life to the faithful, they mean certain death to those who reject the covenant. In the New Covenant, as in the Old, God gives man the choice between life and death, blessing and curse (see Dt 30:19). To choose the covenant is to choose eternal life in God's family. To reject the New Covenant in Christ's blood is to choose one's own death.

Know Pain, Know Gain

How can we square such liturgical wrath with our understanding of the Eucharist as a banquet of love?

We can do so only if we recall that God has revealed Himself as "our Father." That is how we address Him in every Mass: "Our Father, Who art in heaven." In history and in our individual lives, God disciplines as a father disciplines his children (see Heb 12:5–11). No father will stand idly by as his toddler daughter reaches her hands into a hot oven or rotating fan blades. He will call out for her to stop, and he will remove her from proximity to danger. To the child, Daddy's voice might sound harsh and his action seem unjust. A toddler cannot conceive of the perils ahead. She saw only the beckoning light of the burner or the rhythmic beauty of the rotors. She was just beginning to enjoy herself when Daddy took everything away.

Our Father is actively involved in our lives and in history. The Lord disciplines those whom He loves (Heb 12:6; Prv 3:11–12). "God's kindness," said St. Paul, "is meant to lead you to repentance" (Rom 2:4). God often "punishes" us in ways that seem harsh and exceedingly difficult. But even those punishments are remedial. Sometimes nothing short of a personal calamity will make us turn away from our pride, our cruelty, our unwillingness to forgive, our sinful habits, or our excessive love for earthly things.

God's punishments are never vindictive or arbitrary; they are the inevitable consequences of our free choices. Indeed, His punishments are the safeguards of human freedom and assurance of divine love. For no love can be coerced. We must be free to choose God's love or reject it. If God did not permit us to say "no" to Him, our "yes" would be inauthentic and worthless.

When Jesus preached His manifesto, His Sermon on the Mount, He summed up the law of the New Covenant in the sayings we call "The Beatitudes," the "blessings": "Blessed are you poor . . . Blessed are you that hunger . . . Blessed are you that weep" (Lk 6:20–23). They are beautiful, encouraging benedictions. But we must never forget that the Lord followed those blessings with a series of curses: "Woe to you that are rich . . . Woe to you that are full . . . Woe to you that laugh" (vv. 24–26).

It is a hard truth for the modern mind to bear, but it is nonetheless true: We cannot have the balm of the covenant blessing without accepting the sting of the covenant curses. It is a fearsome matter; but the alternative is unbearable, for it would strip us of our freedom and God of His love. A covenant without curses is no covenant at all.

Pageantry or Mystery?

The early Christians knew the stakes involved in the covenant liturgy. They knew the terms they were accepting. They knew the risks. But they also knew that life was unbearable outside God's covenant.

Thus, when they spoke of the Mass, they spoke of its terrifying power, but also its divine promise. In my parish, we sometimes sing a hymn that's translated from the ancient liturgy attributed to the apostle James, the first bishop of Jerusalem. I think that hymn captures well the awe of our Christian ancestors as they renewed their covenant in the Eucharist.

> *Let all mortal flesh keep silence,*
> *And with fear and trembling stand;*
> *Ponder nothing earthly minded,*
> *For with blessing in His hand,*
> *Christ our God to earth descendeth,*
> *Our full homage to demand.*

Christ comes to us with blessings. We stand trembling in awe. That is the faith of God's covenant people.

We still sing those same words from the age of the fathers, but do we hold the same sentiments? Do we experience the Mass the same way? Do we profess the same faith?

In 1994, a *New York Times*/CBS News poll concluded that only 34 percent of Catholics in the United States believe that, in the Mass, the bread and wine become the body and blood of Christ, while 63 percent said that the bread and wine are merely symbolic reminders of Jesus. A 1997 study produced similar results. In most American dioceses, those figures reflect Mass attendance, as well. Though the Church requires us—under penalty of mortal sin—to go to Mass on Sundays and holy days, only a third of us manage to get there.

How strange that, as faith in the sacraments declines, we see an almost hysterical need to pump our liturgical events full of pageantry. A growing number of Catholics spend hundreds and even thousands of dollars to dress up the celebration of confirmation and even first Communion—not to mention matrimony. They buy designer gowns and hire photographers and musicians. They rent a hall and spread a lavish banquet. Yet it's all for nothing if it does not lead us to stand in awe of the covenant of Jesus Christ.

Mass Martyrs

Compare our experience today with the story of the fourth-century martyrs of Abitina, a town in North Africa.

There were fifty of them, ordinary Christians living in the time of the Roman Empire's most sweeping and cruel persecution, that of the emperor Diocletian. And one Sunday, they made themselves easy targets for the authorities. They gathered for Mass.

For their pagan neighbors, Sunday was an ordinary day, a workday like any other. There was no good reason for fifty people to gather together outside the marketplace—unless they were Christians, of course, meeting to swear their oath to their foreign god and eat their covenant meal in secret.

For the Roman guard in Abitina, catching Christians that day was like spearing fish in a barrel. Once they saw the crowd assemble, they just had to wait till the end of the liturgy and then arrest the worshippers en masse.

The day of their trial arrived, and the judge could not believe the apparent stupidity of the Christians. He asked why they would expose themselves in such a way. A lector named Emeritus responded simply: "We cannot live without the Mass." Another man, named Felix, added, "Christians can no more live without the Mass than the Mass can be celebrated without Christians." He concluded: "Christians make the Mass, and the Mass makes Christians. One cannot exist without the other."

These believers were, of course, convicted and sent to their deaths. Could there be any doubt that they were guilty of swearing their oath to Christ, "as to a god"? Indeed, they said they could not live without the oath; life was unimaginable without it. Each and every one of the fifty—men, women, and children—preferred death to missing Mass on a Sunday.

Now, *that* is the power of the oath. These African men and women were, in the most literal sense, martyrs—from the Greek word *martus,* that is, "witnesses"—who gave sworn testimony (*marturia,* "martyrdom") with their very lives. In sacred courts and secular, they were bound by oath to tell the truth, and they did.

That is the power that conquered the mighty empire by the blood of the martyrs and the blood of Jesus Christ— the blood of the new and everlasting covenant. And it is the power that we must allow to reconquer us today.

Because it's true: We cannot live without the Mass. To live without the sacraments is to live apart from the covenant. And such a life is no life at all. In biblical terms, it is the very definition of death.

CHAPTER 12

❧❧❧

SEX, LIES, AND SACRAMENTS

J ESUS TOLD HIS disciples that He had come to light a
fire on the earth, and how He longed for it to be kin-
dled. The name of that fire is the covenant, and the
sacraments fuel its flames as they renew the oath.

This is not the opinion of a theologian. It is the teaching of the Catholic Church, expressed by the Second Vatican Council: "The renewal in the Eucharist of the
covenant between the Lord and man draws the faithful
into the compelling love of Christ and sets them on fire."

The Eucharist is the sacrament of sacraments, the
source and the summit of all Christian life. So any discussion of the sacraments will necessarily dwell on the Mass
most of all.

But the fire of Christ almost always begins with water.
Baptism is the doorway to all the other sacraments. So any
discussion of the sacraments must also linger a while on this
first sacrament of initiation.

Of the seven sacraments, baptism and Eucharist are the
most familiar to us *as sacraments*. Even most breakaway

Christian denominations continue to practice these, in some form, and recognize them as scriptural and essential. And they are right, of course. Baptism and Eucharist are the two principal sacraments that Jesus Himself discussed in terms of stark necessity: "Unless" we receive them, He said, we have no part in His salvation.

This is not to say that God is bound by the rites themselves. The Church has always recognized the possibility of salvation without the covenant rituals. Some people may desire Christ, but die before receiving baptism. Tradition tells us that they are saved by a "baptism of desire." If they die as martyrs for the faith while still preparing for baptism, they are said to undergo a "baptism of blood." Still, the grace they receive is a baptismal grace.

In a similar way, a Christian who desires Holy Communion, but cannot possibly attend Mass (because of distance, for example, or disability), can express this desire in a prayer of "spiritual communion" and receive all the graces of the Eucharist. Still, the grace received is a eucharistic grace.

Baptism and Eucharist are emblematic of all the sacraments, and so they have occupied our attention through much of this book. But we must acknowledge that there are five more sacraments—penance, confirmation, holy orders, anointing of the sick, and marriage—and each of these is a covenant oath worthy of its own book-length study. Now, I would like to dwell for a moment on the sacrament that is most familiar to the world, and even the non-Christian world, but least familiar *as a sacrament*. Yet it is the oath that God Himself favored, throughout the Scriptures, as the most revelatory sign of His covenant with His people.

It is the sacrament of marriage.

Bed Company

The Old Testament speaks of many types of covenants— treaties and truces, adoptions, coronations, and so on— but, by far, the most common type of covenant was marriage. Marriage was a covenant that established a new family relationship between a man and a woman, with God as their witness. Blessings came to those couples who were faithful; curses descended upon those who did not fulfill their covenant oath. When asked why curses had come, the prophet Malachi thundered: "Because the Lord was witness to the covenant between you and the wife of your youth, to whom you have been faithless, though she is your companion and your wife by covenant" (Mal 2:14).

When God wished to describe His covenant relation- ship with Israel, marriage was the metaphor He favored. Through Isaiah, He announced to His people: "Your Maker is your husband" (Is 54:5). Through Ezekiel, the Lord explained how He had courted Israel: "When I passed you again and looked upon you, behold, you were at the age for love . . . I plighted my troth to you and en- tered into a covenant with you, says the Lord God, and you became Mine" (Ezek 16:8). The theme of God's mar- riage covenant with Israel runs throughout the book of the

prophet Hosea. God calls upon Hosea to marry a prosti-
tute—who cheats on him shamelessly—so that his very life
might symbolize Israel's faithlessness to its covenant with
God. Through the prophet Jeremiah, too, God laments
the infidelity of His earthly spouse: "My covenant . . . they
broke, though I was their husband, says the Lord" (Jer
31:32).

The metaphor continues in the New Testament, where
Paul employs it to describe Christ's relationship with the
Church, the Israel of God. "Husbands love your wives, as
Christ loved the Church and gave Himself up for her. . . .
For this reason a man shall leave his father and mother and
be joined to his wife, and the two shall become one flesh.
This mystery is a profound one, and I am saying that it
refers to Christ and the Church" (Eph 5:25, 31–32). St.
Paul's inspired words draw an analogy that we, otherwise,
might hesitate to state. Christ's "one flesh" communion
with His Church—in the ecstasy and intimacy of the
Eucharist—finds its most appropriate analogy in a husband's "one flesh" communion with his wife, in married
sexual love.

Indeed, the act that consummates the covenant is sexual intercourse. The Old Testament is clear on this point.
The law stated in Deuteronomy that if an Israelite man
wished to marry a captive, "you may go in to her, and be
her husband, and she shall be your wife" (Dt 21:13). (To
"go in to" is a Hebrew euphemism for sexual relations.)

Note that they were not husband and wife because
they lived together, or shared meals, or felt a mutual at-

traction. Indeed, the passage assumes that the woman is *already* a captive in the household of the man and presumably *already* shares his table for dinner. But it is the act of making love that changes everything, and it does so by consummating a family bond, a covenant bond.

The act was the fulfillment of the oath. Israelite men customarily ratified the covenant, first, by a verbal pledge. Doing this, the couple demonstrated their consent. But the covenant was not fulfilled or consummated until the moment of their sexual union. The Old Testament provides ample evidence that the moment that binds a man and woman indissolubly is the moment when a man would "go in to" a woman.

Sexual union within marriage, then, is an oath-in-action, a liturgical event. Thus, it is also a sign of something divine.

If married love is a sacramental sign of God's love for His people—as both testaments of the Bible testify—then the act itself must accurately reflect that love. It must be faithful, monogamous, indissoluble, and fruitful. This is the foundation of all traditional Christian sexual morality, though it will surely come as a surprise to many Christians today. I know this, because it took me completely by surprise, some twenty years ago.

Planned Barrenhood

Return with me, for a moment, to the campus I was strolling at the beginning of this book. It was the early 1980s, and Kimberly and I were newlyweds. Ardent Presbyterians, we both were studying theology at a conservative evangelical seminary.

The curriculum was demanding; money was tight; and we, like all our married friends, were using contraceptives. Children would have to wait till we were ready, financially and otherwise. In the meantime, artificial birth control allowed us the pleasure of what we considered "normal" marital relations. We thought of it as an extended honeymoon.

During our second year at seminary, however, Kimberly discovered the lie that was at the root of our married life. In research for an ethics course, she found that, until 1930, Christian churches—without exception—condemned contraception in the strongest terms. The Protestant reformers, whom we revered, went so far as to call it "murder." Kimberly also found out that the anticontraception laws—which were on the books in many states until the 1960s—were largely the work of evangelical Protestant legislators.

Yet Christian history's overwhelming verdict on contraception arrived as news to us, as did the powerful arguments for this teaching from Scripture and moral reasoning. Confronted with the evidence, Kimberly and I felt compelled to change our lives. So we threw the contraceptives away, and soon afterward our change of theology produced a change in Kimberly's anatomy. Our first child, Michael, was on the way.

Signs of Life

Until then, we had lived a lie. It was not until years later, however, when I became a Catholic, that I could understand the true nature of our sin. Pope John Paul II has rightly called contraception "a lie in the language of love." Sex, according to Catholic faith, should be an oath in action, a complete gift of self, an embrace in which a man and a woman hold nothing back from one another. It is a gift of an entire life, and so it belongs only in a lifelong, exclusive marriage. It is a covenant exchange, an exchange of persons: "I am yours, and you are mine." Marriage is what makes sex sacramental and covenantal.

The total gift of self rules out the possibility of divorce, adultery, premarital sex—and contraception. For contracepting couples do hold something back, and it's perhaps the single greatest power two human beings can possess: their fertility, the ability to co-create with God a new life, body and soul, destined for eternity.

The sexual act says in its ecstasy: "I give you everything." But contraception renders that communication untrue.

For sex is a sign, a sacramental sign. Sex is, in the traditional lingo, "*the* marital act," the act that consummates the sacrament of marriage. And a sacrament is a channel of divine grace, which is the very life of God. So when we mess with the "sign" of sex, we're not just changing the way we talk about love; we're ceasing to love. What the novelist Flannery O'Connor said about the Eucharist could well be applied to all the sacraments: If it's just a symbol, then to hell with it.

In sacraments, we incarnate the truth. The word becomes flesh. Thus, for Catholics, sex is a mystery, but it is not something that eludes moral certainty or verifiable reality.

It helps for us to know that the root of the word "sacrament" is the Latin word for "oath." When we make love, we place ourselves under solemn oath—to tell the truth, the whole truth, and nothing but the truth. (So help me, God.) Sexual union is now, as it was in ancient Israel, an oath in action.

And what is the truth we tell under the oath sign of marriage? We say that God is one, and God is a Trinity. The two become one flesh, and soon they are joined by a third; yet they remain one family. Pope John Paul II wrote: "God in His deepest mystery is not a solitude, but a family, since He has in Himself fatherhood, sonship, and the essence of the family, which is love." And the *Catechism* adds: "The communion of the Holy Trinity is the source and criterion of truth in every relationship" (n. 2845).

By God's design, marriage is the only relationship that reveals the life-giving power of love. Human love, with its fruitfulness, vividly manifests God's own being and inner life. Marriage is a sacramental sign of the Trinitarian life we hope to share forever in heaven: "In the joys of their love and family life [God] gives them here on earth a foretaste of the wedding feast of the Lamb" (CCC, n. 1642; see also Rev 19:9).

All that is the truth we tell with our bodies.

We tell, too, that God is faithful to His people. Again, marital intimacy is the metaphor St. Paul chose to apply to Christ and the Church. The Book of Revelation, in the original language, is "the book of unveiling" *(apokalupsis)*—which was a euphemism for a couple's first consummation of their marriage.

Marriage, then, is not only a sacrament; it is a sacramental sign of the other sacraments and the life they give (see CCC, n. 1617).

The Oath for Both

It all begins with the oath. The sacred oath doesn't make marital fidelity easy, but it does make it possible. Lifelong love is a many-splendored thing, but it also has an element of fear and trembling to it, because it is within a covenantal context that we'll be working out our salvation (see Phil 2:13).

Marriage makes two lives so interconnected, so intimate, so intensely involved with one another—so danger-ously vulnerable to one another—that both the man and woman *must* be placed under oath. Remember: For the sake of the common good, we don't trust police officers or soldiers to carry guns until they're sworn in, when God's abiding presence is accessible to them at each and every temptation. How much more should this be true of mar-riage and sex. It isn't romanticism or idealism to believe that sex should be saved for marriage. Sex, with its fear-some intimacy and mutual vulnerability, is demanding enough for those who are committed to a lifetime to-gether. It's unrealistic idealism to think that anyone can sustain that level of trust and intimacy without a sacrament, a covenant bond, an abiding presence of God.

CHAPTER 13

❧❧❧

THE SACRED
REALM OF RISK

SOMETIMES I FEEL as if I'm always telling the story of my love for my wife, Kimberly. Even when I'm writing works of theology, I keep coming back to the love story that matters most to me. Sometimes, when I read the Scriptures, I think that God must feel the same way.

As a student, I burned with a love of truth. Kimberly's beauty opened my eyes to the truth of love. It was her loving witness that lifted me out of my boredom with the sacraments; and it was that realization that eventually allowed me to see Kimberly's body and its beauty as something sacramental. I always knew she was beautiful; but, once we put contraception aside, her body—with its cycles of life—appeared to me as a mystery. I felt not just desire for her, but awe before her and greater awe before the God Who made us. Together, we had stepped decisively into the covenant, into the sacred realm of risk.

I know now that all those moments were graces of our marriage sacrament—blessings of the marriage covenant.

Still, I don't want to give the impression that married

life has been a sort of dazed euphoria for us, punctuated only by moments of sudden and brilliant illumination. That isn't how covenant works. That isn't what blessing means.

In fact, if we search the Scriptures, we will find that every covenant came with a test, a trial; and, without exception, God's chosen people failed the test. It was true of Adam, Noah, Abraham, Moses, and David. You can be sure that it is true of you and me, as well. As we attempt to live up to our covenants—our baptismal vocation to holiness, our marital vocation to purity, and so on—we will be tested, and we will find ourselves unable to pass the test.

Tried and True

For Kimberly and me, the trial came, strangely enough, as a direct result of her heroic witness to me. She had convinced me of the importance of the sacraments. She had convinced me of the wrongness of contraception. But these two victories had led me, in turn, to examine more closely the claims of the Church that consistently upheld the realism of the sacraments and the immorality of artificial birth control. That was the Catholic Church, which I had, until then, held in contempt. At first, I wondered whether these instances of Catholic fidelity were dumb luck or an ingenious counterfeit of the devil. I did not see Catholicism as a serious threat to my convictions, and so I went on to accept ordination as a Presbyterian minister.

But I kept reading; and, as I looked into Catholic doctrines one by one, I found that they were all firmly grounded in the Scriptures. And they held together better than any Protestant system I had known.

Again and again, I felt the excitement of new discovery. The Eucharist, the intercession of saints, the papacy: All of these things I had once viewed as unscriptural innovations, I now saw as the fruit of the biblical covenants. With each discovery, I would rush to tell Kimberly what I had found, reading aloud to her from catechisms, papal encyclicals, and the works of the Church fathers and medieval saints. Kimberly, however, did not share my enthusiasm. She began to fear that I would convert, and I was afraid she was right.

More each day, I looked to the Catholic Church and saw truth, goodness, and beauty—even as I grew more grateful to my evangelical Protestant formation for all it taught me about the covenant. I tried to show all this to Kimberly, but she could not see it. She did not want to see it. All she could see was her every dream crashing down around her.

She had planned her life so well. She wanted to marry a minister. Her father was a minister. Her uncle was a minister. Two of her brothers were on their way to the ministry. And her husband was a minister, but he was fading fast.

It became clear to me that I could no longer function as a Protestant pastor. To do so would be to live a lie. So I resigned from my ministry in 1983, and from my job as a seminary professor, and I moved my family to another job (for less pay) in another state.

Communication Breakdown

Kimberly took all of this very hard. Not only had I left behind the faith of her fathers, I had also uprooted the family and plunged us into some financial hardship. She no longer was willing to listen when I spoke of my Catholic discoveries. She was not at all bitter, resentful, or hostile. She was heartbroken. She struggled mightily with despair. Our communication had almost completely broken down.

More than once, late at night, I heard her sobbing softly into her pillow in our darkened bedroom. She confessed to me that she had prayed God would give her a fatal illness, so that she could find peace and I could move on with my life. At one point, she even left for a week, to get perspective on the situation and to pray with a couple who were friends of ours from seminary. She hoped that they could help her find ways to overturn my discoveries and turn me back to the faith we had shared.

I felt as if I were on a boat (the barque of Peter) that was pulling away from the shore where Kimberly stood, determined, resolute.

Still, she knew that I had to do what I discerned as God's will. So she acquiesced when I told her I would be received into the Church on Easter Vigil 1986. She even asked if she could attend the Mass with me. This made me so happy, but even that was bittersweet, as I walked up, alone, to receive my first Communion. I still remember the prayer I prayed when I returned to my seat beside Kimberly. I put my arm around her, though she seemed so far away. In my heart I said: *Jesus, why would You show me Your bride and then have it drive my bride so far from me? Why would You show me Your family and have it drive a wedge into my family?*

If not for Kimberly's firm belief in the marriage covenant, she surely would have left me. But she knew, she told me years later, that she could not leave me without leaving God, as well. She would ask God to help her through the next ten minutes, and then ten minutes more, and then ten minutes more.

I continued to keep silent about spiritual and theological matters, as did Kimberly. This was difficult for a devout couple who had been trained together for the ministry. But now we seemed to have so little in common; so what we did share we tended to emphasize. We focused on our love for our children. And we renewed our attention to physical affection and intimacy. In time, God blessed that intimacy, and we conceived a child, and thus we drew close in the ways that we could.

Midway through the pregnancy, however, Kimberly began to hemorrhage badly. We rushed to the hospital, where the doctors determined that our baby was in a position of placenta previa, making the pregnancy difficult to sustain. They controlled the bleeding, and Kimberly was able to return home; but she would be confined to bed for most of the next four months.

I know couples who have faced unspeakable illnesses, illnesses that would issue forth not in life, but in the death of a spouse or a child. What they have endured is harder, but what we went through in that pregnancy was harder than anything we had known.

Our common hopes and fears drew us still closer. And, since Kimberly's condition required sexual abstinence, we found new ways of intimacy. I gave history's longest backrubs.

The birth of our daughter Hannah proved to be a big breakthrough. I was not going to impose my will regarding the baby's baptism, but Kimberly came to me and stunned me by saying that she wanted Hannah to be baptized in the faith of her father. To my amazement, Kimberly not only attended the baptism, but found herself drawn into the liturgy. The prayers had her standing on tiptoe, saying "Amen!" and "Alleluia!" at all the right times.

Hannah's baptism was a celebration of new life that came from our love. Kimberly would eventually see that moment as the beginning of an astonishing time of grace—a span of several years that would culminate in her conversion in 1990. (But that's another story, another book.)

All told, we faced a seven-year trial of our marriage covenant. I know of marriages that *seemed* stronger—seemed blissful, in fact—but did not survive. I know of marriages that seemed weaker than ours, but have endured and come out stronger. What makes the difference between success and failure? I believe it was only the grace of the sacrament. We received the grace when we honored the covenant, by calling upon the Name of the Lord, again and again and again.

The grace of matrimony enabled us to go through a terrible trial and come out with a love supernaturally refined and stronger than ever. Today, I thank God for the pain and the tears and the struggles.

Fear Factor

No less than Adam and Noah, Abraham and Moses, you and I will find our faithfulness tested and tried.

God does not force anyone to love or obey Him. He allows us a choice. He placed Adam and Eve in a garden full of delights and invited them to partake of any tree but one. "Of the tree of the knowledge of good and evil you shall not eat," God commanded, "for in the day that you eat of it you shall die" (Gen 2:17).

Temptation came in the form of a deadly beast with angelic intelligence. The serpent undermined Adam and Eve's trust in God. They feared him, but they were too proud to cry out for help. So they sinned, and they failed the test that God had permitted for their good.

If they had feared God more than they feared the serpent, they would have chosen martyrdom, and they would have entered into a life even greater than paradise. By offering a complete sacrifice of their lives, they would have fulfilled the covenant and begun to live the life of the Trinity. For God is love, and love demands a total gift of self. In eternity, the complete gift of self is the Trinity's inner life. In time, the image of divine life is *sacrificial, life-giving* love. We must die to ourselves for the sake of another. And that's what Adam and Eve failed to do.

Temptation's Greatest Hits

Everyone must face the great test.

Why does God allow trials? Because only through trials do we recognize our weakness and our need. When we suffer, we soon find the limits of our endurance and the paucity of our resources. We're not strong enough to make it. We're not smart enough. We don't have what it takes. We're in over our heads. We simply cannot be trusted to remain faithful to our vocation.

But God will not allow us to be tested beyond our endurance (see 1 Cor 10:13). And He will be faithful. All we need do is call on His name, as we do implicitly in every oath. When we ask God's help, we will receive His grace, and that is all we need in order to persevere.

The early Christian writer Origen once wrote: "There is a certain usefulness to temptation." Temptation, when resisted, strengthens the believer. Indeed, God permits trials for this reason. Temptation makes us face the stark choice: for God or against God. When we make the decision for God, we grow stronger in faith, hope, and love. St. James tells us: "Blessed is the man who endures trial, for when he has stood the test he will receive the crown of life which God has promised to those who love Him" (Jas 1:12).

All of God's "favorites" were tempted by severe trials. Consider Abraham, who was asked to sacrifice his only son. Consider Joseph, who was beaten and sold into slavery by his own brothers. Consider Job, whose family and property perished in Satan's murderous rampage. Above all, consider Jesus; for God did not spare Him the most severe temptations. If Jesus Himself had to face the temptations of the devil, we should not complain that we are unloved when God permits us to be tried. Like God's other beloved, we will shine more brightly when we have struggled successfully with God's help. "God tested them and found them worthy of Himself; like gold in the furnace He tried them, and like a sacrificial burnt offering He accepted them. In the time of their visitation they will shine forth" (Wis 3:5–7).

Weak Need

Though trials lay us low, we must never cease calling on God's name. Our help is in the *name* of the Lord, who made heaven and earth. We are His family by covenant, and so He has given us His name as our own. Thus, we have the right and sometimes the duty to call upon that name for help. Should our personal lives—or even our cities and our homes—fall into ruin, we must call on His mercy and fall on His mercy.

His power is made perfect in our weakness. Consider how God fulfilled His covenant with Israel. Twice in ten years, the armies of Babylon had swept into the land of Judah. They had left Jerusalem and the Temple in smoldering rubble, and they returned to their country with thousands of captives, including most of the country's elites and tradesmen. Of the twelve tribes that had once made up the great nation of Israel, only a remnant of two tribes would return, some decades later. And, as the generations passed, it seemed impossible that God could ever do as He promised and restore all the tribes to their promised land.

It was a low point of the history of the chosen people. Yet God chose that moment to offer them His greatest consolation: "I will make a new covenant with the house of Israel and the house of Judah, not like the covenant which I made with their fathers. . . . My covenant which they broke . . . But this is the covenant which I will make with the house of Israel after those days, says the Lord: I will put my law within them, and I will write it upon their hearts; and I will be their God, and they shall be My people" (Jer 31: 31–33).

Humiliations humble us; and God finds humility irresistible. We may not see our nation reduced to rubble; but we will nonetheless find many opportunities to grow in humility. St. Therese of Lisieux defined this virtue in a homey way, as humbly accepting and patiently enduring our own weaknesses.

Reverse Curse

This is the covenant we know in the sacraments. God writes His law into our lives; He writes His law of self-giving love onto our hearts; He gives us His strength so that we need not rely on our own.

This is the blessing we know when we accept the oath, and it is a hard blessing. In the Old Covenant, God promised His people land and wealth and progeny, if only they would be faithful. He gave them what they wanted so that they would trust Him. And once they trusted Him, He sought to show them what they *really* needed. But instead of trusting Him, they sought their satisfaction in their land and wealth and power and progeny.

The promised rewards of the Old Covenant were earthly signs of heavenly realities—the only rewards that can truly satisfy the human heart's deepest longing. In the New Covenant, God gives us not what we want, but what we need. We can trust Him to give us "every good endowment and every perfect gift" (Jas 1:17), according to our deepest needs.

We must always trust in God and never let our doubts overtake us. We will certainly mourn in life and ache because we lack or have lost the good things of God's creation. We will find ourselves losing more of them every day, through aging, illness, the vagaries of the stock market, the death of friends and family members. But all these things are—like the land and wealth and progeny of the Old Covenant—just earthly reflections of the heavenly love we truly need.

If we seek our rest in the gifts, we will never find rest. If we look beyond the gifts to the Giver, we will know everlasting peace, even amid the most terrifying difficulties of life. "But whatever gain I had I counted as loss for the sake of Christ. Indeed I count everything as loss because of the surpassing worth of knowing Christ Jesus my Lord. For His sake I have suffered the loss of all things, and count them as dung, in order that I may gain Christ" (Phil 3:8).

Loss is gain, and gain is loss! The New Covenant has reversed the polarity on the blessings and curses of the Old Covenant. In the Beatitudes, Jesus declared the poor blessed and the rich accursed. Our Lord Himself became the most "accursed" man of all by the terms of the Old Covenant. "Christ redeemed us from the law, having become a curse for us" (Gal 3:13). In an ironic fulfillment that crowns all the narrative twists of the Old Testament, we are saved by a curse pronounced in God's law: "Cursed be every one who hangs on a tree" (Dt 21:23). We are saved by the suffering brought on by our sin!

We must learn to appreciate how much of our religion rests on this understanding of the oath, the covenant, the curse, and the incarnation of God. When Muslim theologians dispute the plausibility of the Genesis account of God's covenant with Abraham, they point out two reasons why God could never have sworn an oath: (1) God is almighty and has no one greater to swear by; and (2) God is unchanging and eternal, and so He cannot bear a curse.

Yet, for Christians, it is His divine nature itself that guarantees the oath. Both the Old Testament and the New report that God swore by Himself (see Gen 22:16, Heb 6:13). "So when God desired to show more convincingly to the heirs of the promise the unchangeable character of His purpose He interposed with an oath" (Heb 6:17). Moreover, because of the incarnation, God has sent "His own Son in the likeness of sinful flesh and for sin" (Rom 8:3). The very reason for the incarnation was so that God could bear the covenant curse for us. "For our sake He made Him to be sin Who knew no sin, so that in Him we might become the righteousness of God" (2 Cor 5:21).

Sealed with a Curse

The first Christians knew the meaning of covenant so well that they identified Christ, most reverently, with the curse. The earliest sacramental manual, the *Didache,* closes with a reference to an inevitable "fiery trial of testing" in which "many shall be offended and perish; but those who endure in their faith shall be saved by the Curse Himself" (16:5).

Like all of God's beloved, we will be tested. Indeed, such testing is the common lot of mankind. But "God is faithful, and He will not let you be tempted beyond your strength, but with the temptation will also provide the way of escape, that you may be able to endure it" (1 Cor 10:13). We need never fail in our fidelity to the covenant, as did our ancestors long ago. We may not receive lands and wealth as our reward, but we will receive grace—divine life—which is greater than any other gift.

Everything we need, we receive in the sacraments. This is God's work, unmerited by us. Sacraments don't make life easy, but they do make it possible. They divinize us, and so they take us a long way upward. But then it's a long way down if we fall.

What else could Jesus have meant in that curious passage in Mark's gospel, when two beloved disciples ask Him for a place of honor in His kingdom? He asks James and John: "Are you able to drink the cup that I drink, or to be baptized with the baptism with which I am baptized?" (Mk 10:38). His question assumes a covenant sealed by sacraments—Eucharist and baptism, the chalice and the bath—and tested in a trial by ordeal. Sacraments are not a way out of suffering; they are the only way *through* suffering: suffering in union with Jesus Christ.

Our Lord counseled us: "Fear is useless. What is needed is trust" (Lk 8:50). We must always trust in God. He has sworn an oath, and He has sworn with His own name as surety. If we feel weak, we need only call out His name. And we *should* feel weak, because we are. If we feel that we can't bear our suffering, if we feel that we're in over our heads, then that means we're getting a clearer view of reality. "Apart from Me," Jesus told His disciples, "you can do nothing" (Jn 15:5). St. Paul, however, added the necessary corollary when he said: "I can do all things in Him Who strengthens me" (Phil 4:13).

It is a dangerous thing to place oneself under oath; but it is far more dangerous not to do so. "It is a fearful thing to fall into the hands of the living God" (Heb 10:31); but it is a more fearful thing, and an ultimately damnable thing, to fall anywhere else. For we are already in a trial by ordeal. We are in a fight for our lives.

God's sacraments have borne us this far, and they can bear us the rest of the way home.

CHAPTER 14

REAL PRESENCES

ALMOST EVERY MONDAY, very late at night, I grab my jacket and car keys and drive through dark, deserted streets to reach the parking lot of my parish church. St. Peter's has a special entrance, never closed, that gives people round-the-clock access to a basement chapel. It is an adoration chapel—that is, a sanctuary for the sort of praise, petition, and confession that we may address only to God.

This basement room is specially suited for adoration, and not just because God is in every place and this is a quiet place. This chapel is right for adoration because God is here, sacramentally present. In the adoration chapel, worshippers may, at any hour of the day or night, gaze upon the Eucharist, exposed in a golden monstrance. And there is Jesus: purest white against the most radiant gold. There—to use the language of devotional love—is His real presence in the Blessed Sacrament: body, blood, soul, and divinity.

It's my custom to spend an hour in this chapel once a

week. Tradition calls such a time of prayer, spent before the Blessed Sacrament, a "holy hour." I love those hours. They are blissfully unguarded moments. In the silence, I pour out my heart to Jesus. I read the Scriptures in the company of their Author. I read my own writings to Him, too, from rough drafts or from my journals. I tell Jesus about each of my children, one by one. I ask Him what I need to change in my life, so that I may serve them and serve Him better. I ask Him to give me courage to face the trials that inevitably come to my life. And I wait quietly for His word.

Holy hours are my oases of peace and joy, and much-needed moments of catharsis. They are the times when I am most myself, because I know that I can hide nothing— not my sins, my desires, or my motives—from God, Who is really present with me.

If the Eucharist is my covenant oath, then my holy hour is the time when I contemplate that oath, with all its promise and with all its demands. It is a fearful thing, a thrilling thing. (Did I really once believe that sacraments were boring?)

Rapt Presence

Jesus' presence in the Eucharist is unique. The early Church used a certain Greek word to describe this reality. They called it *parousia,* which means "presence, arrival, coming, or advent." Today, non-Catholics (and even many Catholics) use the word *parousia* to denote the so-called second coming of Christ at the end of time—distinct from His daily coming in the Eucharist. It was not so, however, in the works of the Church fathers and in the earliest liturgies; there, "Eucharist" and "second coming" are often treated as equivalent events.

This was a commonplace to Christians of the first, second, and third centuries; and, to scholars of history—whether Catholic or not—the notion appears so pervasive as to be obvious. The great historical theologian Jaroslav Pelikan, writing as a Lutheran, observed of the early Church: "The coming of Christ was 'already' and 'not yet': He had come already—in the incarnation, and on the basis of the incarnation would come in the Eucharist; He had come already in the Eucharist, and would come at the last in the new cup that He would drink with them in His Father's kingdom." Pelikan concludes: "The eucharistic liturgy was not a compensation for the postponement of the *parousia,* but a way of celebrating the presence of one who had promised to return."

Though a final *parousia* will one day come, the Eucharist is the *parousia* here and now. What the ancients saw in the liturgy was the coming of Christ; and what they meant by *parousia* is what we today should mean by the real presence.

That is the presence we know in the Eucharist. It is a powerful reality, full of Christ's heavenly glory, though we cannot yet *see* Him in all His glory. This real, substantial, divine presence is what makes our oath, our *sacramentum,* possible and valid.

Real to Real

Again, the Eucharist is unique. It is *the* Blessed Sacrament. It is *the* real presence. But it is not the only blessed sacrament. And it is not the only sacrament in which we find Him really present.

He is present also in the covenant bond of marriage. Indeed, it was His name we invoked when we made our vows, His help Kimberly and I enlisted and His protection, for the sake of His promise. It is His presence that makes the covenant binding. Jesus Christ abides in our marriage, in a real way, for as long as we both shall live. A good friend of mine refers to this as "the real presence of the marital bond."

All theological ideas have consequences. All Christian doctrines imply some deep call to conversion of our lives. Long ago, I considered Jesus' real presence in my marriage—His sacramental presence—and I asked our Lord how I might better live out this truth. And I made a resolution to Him. I told Him that, just as I dutifully scheduled my weekly hour before the Blessed Sacrament of the altar, so I would also begin to schedule regular time before the *blessed sacrament of the hearth.* I would make more time for Kimberly.

Yes, the Eucharist is *the* Blessed Sacrament, but Kimberly is *a* blessed sacrament for me. Some Catholics tend to think of the Eucharist as the only flesh-and-blood sacrament, in contrast with marriage, which they proceed to overspiritualize. But marriage is a sacrament not merely in some ethereal or abstract way. It is a sacrament in the most complete, body-and-soul way possible.

Kimberly is not only my vocation; she is the minister of the sacrament to me, as I am the minister of the sacrament to her. She is a blessed sacrament, and an hour with her is an hour of prayer, in some ways like the holy hour before the tabernacle at church. I do not worship her as I worship God, and so our house is not in any sense an adoration chapel. But my conversation with her is a sacramental contemplation. In her I see, reflected, the love of the Holy Spirit and the reality of the Church. In our bodily union, I contemplate something of the communion of Christ with His own bride, the Church.

Since marriage is a sacrament, family life is a kind of domestic liturgy, with its own responses, antiphons, and times of silence. There are lines we must never tire of repeating: "Thank you," "I'm sorry," "I love you," "I forgive you," "Tell me about your day," "I'd be glad to do that," and "How about a date?"

At Mass we know how to respond when the priest says, "Lift up your hearts" or "Lord, have mercy" or "Let us proclaim the mystery of faith." In a similar way, we need to learn the responses of the domestic liturgy. When one of us says, "I'm sorry," the other replies, "I forgive you." This liturgy, like any sacramental liturgy, is not something mechanical or magical, but rather a habit-forming pattern of love. We don't always feel the emotions when we say the words, at Mass or at home; but if we are sincere, God makes up for what we lack.

It is for me, and me alone, that Kimberly's presence is a sacramental presence of Jesus Christ. Kimberly is the embodiment of my divine vocation, and no one else's. Yet marriage is not merely a private sacrament. It is not just an inward reality for couples only. Marriage is a sacrament of the Church, and it is an *outward* sign of any inward grace received by the couple. A married couple shows the world that God is faithful forever; that He is loving and merciful; that He is lavish in His fruitfulness; and much more, as well.

Marriage is a ministry, too. It is the clear teaching of the Church that baptized spouses are the ordinary ministers of the sacrament of matrimony. Our ministry, however, is essentially different from the ministry of ordained priests. For most Catholics, married life itself will be the only "sermon" we ever get to "preach," and most of it will be wordless. It will be a lasting statement to an unbelieving world, a world that finds fidelity impossible to believe.

All this comes as a consequence of the "real presence" of Jesus Christ in the marital bond. And all of this teaches us, in turn, something more about the real presence of Jesus Christ in the Eucharist. The *parousia* of Christ in the Eucharist is something that needs to be discovered—as a marital bond between the divine Bridegroom with His bride, the Church—the marriage supper of the Lamb. It wouldn't be a marriage if it were just symbolic. Like my marriage to Kimberly, Holy Communion consummates a one-flesh union that is lasting and life-giving.

To Know a Veil

Marriage and the other sacraments are mutually interpretive. The one helps us to understand all the others, and all the others help us to understand the one. Indeed, all the sacraments have a marital dimension.

When we go forward to receive the sacraments, what is really happening? In the midst of all the visible actions, there is an invisible action that is divine. Heaven and earth are united. God and man are united. With Christ as the minister of the sacrament, the New Covenant draws all of us into lasting communion.

"What God has joined together, let not man put asunder" (Mt 19:6). God joins things that seem unjoinable: God and man, heaven and earth, male and female, the law and liturgy. How can these things be combined with any degree of stability?

Only through the divine power of the oath! Christ, by means of the sacraments, reunites these things that humankind has repeatedly and willfully divided. He wants all the world to be taken up into His liturgy, for all the earth to enter into nuptial harmony with heaven.

This bridal unveiling has already taken place. The Gospel of Matthew tells us that, when Jesus died, "the veil of the Temple was torn in two, from top to bottom"

(27:51). Jesus' redemption unveiled the Holy of Holies, opening God's presence to everyone. Heaven and earth could now embrace in intimate love. *We* are the bride of Christ unveiled; *we* are His Church. And Jesus wants each and every one of us to enter into the most intimate relationship imaginable with Him, through the covenantal bond that is consummated in the sacraments. He uses wedding imagery to demonstrate how much He loves us, how close He wants us to stay—and how permanent he intends our union to be. To prepare for this Communion, we must, like any spouses, leave our old lives behind. As bride, we will forsake our old name for a new one. Marriage demands that spouses make a self-sacrifice that is complete and total, as Christ's was on the cross, as Christ's sacrifice remains in the Eucharist.

We celebrate the Eucharist. We celebrate our marriage. Every day, we live out what we celebrate by sacrificing ourselves in love, just like our eucharistic Lord.

Through the Church's sacraments, heaven and earth enter into marriage. That's good news for us—it couldn't be better—but we must always keep in mind that marriage isn't just a honeymoon. It is a trial, too, and that is why it requires an oath.

We have good news to share, but it's daunting news. Everyone we know and everyone we'll ever meet has been called by God, from all eternity, to baptism, to divine life, to be a saint. What will sainthood mean to them? What will it mean to us? Most of us won't face beasts in the Colosseum, or persecution from hostile governments. We will, instead, find our trials close to home, where the goodness of the world is apparent, but so are the sins of fallen nature.

Yet it is in that context that the sacraments are rendered intrinsically powerful. Home is like paradise: It falls down, it falls hard, but in the end it falls back on God's promise in the covenant, and it is raised up to the marriage supper of the Lamb.

CHAPTER 15

❧❦

STRETCHING TOWARD
INFINITY

WHY DO WE swear an oath? Why do we make a covenant?

Because that is what people have always done; that is what people *need* to do.

In domestic families, parents give sacrificially, motivated by the natural bonds of affection and kinship. Even the wicked know how to give good gifts to their children (Mt 7:11). A household, however, must live among many other households; and so, together, these families must extend familial duties to people outside the family. In the larger society, some citizens must assume parental roles such as governing, rendering judgment, administering punishment, and overseeing finances. Since these people cannot rely on natural bonds, society binds them securely with an oath. The oath invokes God's watchful presence and His assistance, to enable people to do what they could not do otherwise. The oath extends a family bond beyond the natural limits of blood, marriage, and adoption.

Contracts are useful for making a marketplace operate

efficiently. But only covenants can secure the trust that goes with kinship. And there are times when that trust is essential. Human society has always placed its citizens under oath as they entered a trial, for example, or prepared for battle.

If all this is true in the human family and human society, then how much more will it be true in the family of God, the divine society we call the Church?

For the world is a trial; the world is our battlefield. G. K. Chesterton said that the Christian life is not hard; it's just humanly impossible. A famous rock singer observed that no one here gets out alive.

Both were right, in a purely natural sense. We cannot truly live, we cannot survive the world, we cannot be saved, without God. We can be saved only if God Himself is with us—as He is, really present, when we call upon Him in our sacred oaths, the sacraments.

The sacraments do not spare us from the trials and the battles, but they give us the only means to come through the trials and battles alive. The sacraments don't make life easy, but they do make it possible. And *only they* can make it possible.

They're not something merely pleasant or convenient. Nor are they mere objects of devotion. We should think of them, instead, as means of survival—like a life preserver, radiation therapy, a respirator—something a person in mortal danger cannot live without.

The Sacramental Gospel

We have a need that only the sacraments can fulfill. God made us that way, and He took on flesh for that very reason. John's gospel shows, with stunning clarity, the providential correspondence between the depth of human need and the superabundance of divine power in the sacraments. "He came to His own home, and His own people received Him not. But to all who received Him, who believed in His name, He gave power to become children of God; who were born, not of blood nor of the will of the flesh nor of the will of man, but of God" (Jn 1:11–13).

We must receive Jesus, and we must believe in His name, if we wish to gain the "power to become children of God."

Even that, however, is not quite enough. The very next chapter of the gospel carries the theme forward, using the very same words. When Jesus went to Jerusalem for the Passover, John tells us, "many" people received Him and "believed in His name," and yet "Jesus did not trust Himself to them" (Jn 2:23–24).

They received Him. They believed in His name. Why didn't Jesus "trust Himself to them"?

John answers the question: Jesus withheld His saving grace "because He knew all men and needed no one to bear witness of man; for He Himself knew what was in man" (Jn 2:25). Three times in a very short space John used the word "man" (in Greek, *anthropos,* or its plural). What he seems to be saying is that human nature—"what was in man"—by itself, is not capable of attaining eternal life. It's not enough for someone to receive and believe. Even our best efforts can't save us.

So what more can a man do?

John shows us in the very next verse, when he uses the word "man" a fourth time. There we meet "a man . . . named Nicodemus," a renowned teacher of the Jews. John would have us understand that this "man" is "everyman"—everyone who lives and breathes.

Nicodemus receives Jesus and believes in His name. Yet Jesus calls him to something more, an ultimate step in the process of conversion—and now He names it: "Truly, truly, I say to you, unless one is born of water and the Spirit, he cannot enter the kingdom of God" (Jn 3:5).

What Jesus said to Nicodemus, He says to every man, woman, and child in subsequent history. Yes, we must believe in His name. Yes, we must receive Him into our hearts. But then we must take the final step. Salvation is not just the matter of a private act. It culminates in an action that is public, liturgical, and sacramental. Without the *sacrament of baptism*—without all the sacraments of Jesus Christ—we cannot hold the power, we cannot enter the kingdom, we cannot even know what it means to be a child of God.

Scholars and saints speak of John's gospel as a "sacramental" gospel; and so it is, from the very beginning. John states the principle in chapter 1, illustrates it in chapter 2, and exemplifies it in chapter 3. Then, as if to add an unmistakable flourish, he takes us immediately from Jesus' nighttime conversation with Nicodemus to a scene that is as clear as a summer day: "After this Jesus and His disciples went into the land of Judea; there He remained with them and baptized" (Jn 3:22).

Setting a President

In swearing the oath, in celebrating the sacraments, we follow after Jesus. As the "pioneer" of our salvation (Heb 2:10ff), He has triumphed through suffering and even death. Jesus is "pioneer and perfecter of our faith" (Heb 12:2), and ours is a sacramental faith. We celebrate the sacraments because Christ did, and because through them He wants to perfect us in faith. In the sacraments, we imitate Christ.

Think of an analogy from the natural order. If you've ever attended a baseball game, you know about the seventh-inning stretch: the moment, late in the game, when players pause their action so that the fans can stand up and stretch their legs. According to American folklore, the custom began in the early twentieth century, when U.S. President William Howard Taft—a six-foot-two, 330-pound behemoth of a man—could no longer endure the stricture of his narrow seat. He stood up; and, following protocol, the entire assembly stood, too. When he resumed his seat, so did everyone else.

As goes the leader, so goes the nation. The seventh-inning stretch has been part of America's national pastime ever since.

Move from the ridiculous to the sublime, and you'll see that this is a deeply ingrained pattern in human nature. Abraham circumcised his son, and so did his faithful off-spring for millennia afterward. Abraham practiced animal sacrifice, and so did his descendants; he offered animal sacrifice at Mount Moriah, and so would his people when they built the Jerusalem Temple (see 2 Chr 3:1)

The actions of the founder—the pioneer, the leader of the nation—redound through the ages. This is how covenants are made. This is how covenants are renewed in every generation.

Jesus was baptized, and so we are baptized. Jesus broke bread and blessed a cup of wine, commanding His followers to "do this" in His memory—and so we do. Jesus gave His Spirit to His disciples to confirm them in faith, and so does the true Church of Christ in our time. Jesus ordained His apostles to celebrate Mass and forgive sins; and so does the Church today. Jesus forgave and healed people in sacramental ways, and so does the Catholic Church. Jesus blessed marriage, and so we, too, count our marriages as blessed and sacramental.

He swore an oath; He made a covenant. And He gave us the sacraments so that we might follow Him, swearing the oath, renewing the covenant forever.

It is thus that He becomes truly our "pioneer and perfecter," divinizing us, calling us "brethren" and sanctifying us (Heb 2:11)—literally, making us saints by the power of the sacraments. It is Jesus Who calls us to be saints (Heb 3:1), and Jesus Who empowers us to be saints, again through the power of the sacraments.

For All *the Saints*

What divine madness: God has called us not to be saintly but to be saints. For only saints will enter heaven. And what is a saint? A saint is someone who has been perfected. "Be perfect," Jesus told the motley crowd that gathered to hear Him. "Be perfect as your heavenly Father is perfect."

These are the terms of the covenant. No one understood this as well as St. Paul, who repeatedly called Christians saints (see, for example, Col 1:2–3). Why does Paul refer to living believers as "saints"? It was not because they behaved better than you and I back in those days. In other letters, Paul accuses the Christians of his day of pretty much all the sins Christians can commit today.

So why does he call ordinary Christians "the holy ones"? Why does he call them "saints"?

Simply because they, like us, have received the sacraments, and so they have received the holiness of Christ from Christ Himself. They have been sanctified, and so they are saints.

Sainthood is not the vocation of an elite corps—the handful of exotics who have been canonized and cast in plaster by the Church. Sainthood is our duty every day. It is our choice of the blessing rather than the curse. Sainthood is the boldest, most outlandish thing we can attempt. It is our reaching into the very life of the Trinity and taking it as our own.

Thus it is a risky business.

No, it's beyond that. It's an impossible dream.

Yet God Himself has called us to sainthood, to perfection, and to a share in His life. God is not cruel. He would not call us to something we could not achieve. And God cannot lie. He Himself is the ground of all truth. Our God is all-powerful. God can and does make finite beings capable of the infinite—*finitum capax infinitum.*

With such a God, even impossible dreams become attainable hopes. For He Himself has attained them for us. A father can reach where a small child cannot. A father will stoop down to give gifts, just to see a child happy. And sainthood is the only thing that can make us happy, either here on earth or forever in heaven. The alternative, which we know too well, is sin and the misery that comes in its wake.

But God divinizes us; the Father shares His own endless happiness with children who have done nothing to deserve it! This is the fatherly provision celebrated in the Scriptures' great unveiling of God's sworn promise in chapter 6 of the Letter to the Hebrews. We should read that chapter often and savor it. It speaks with the confidence that small children have in a loving parent: "the full assurance of hope," "Surely I will bless you," "a sure and steadfast anchor of the soul."

Holiness is unattainable. Yet our Father gives it to us,

if we reach upward and ask for it. We are by nature incapable of the infinite, but He is by nature incapable of failing His children, and that should trump all our fears.

Our sainthood, our holiness, our perfection is ours for the asking. We can be certain of this: "I am sure that He Who began a good work in you will bring it to completion at the day of Jesus Christ" (Phil 1:5). The sacraments themselves are our surety. We do not make the sacraments; they make us. They are God's oath made permanent—abiding signs of His covenant with us—His enduring promise and His almighty power!

We sing it in the Mass today, as our ancestors in faith sang it in the liturgy of ancient, earthly Jerusalem: "The Lord will remember His covenant forever!" May that melody be ever in our minds and hearts. May we never forget to call upon the oath God has sworn—may we never forget to call forth the graces of the sacraments. They are ours by inheritance!

May we never forget till the day when we can no longer forget the covenant, till the day we enjoy the blessings of the covenant forever, in the land of the living, the land of the promise.

SOURCES AND
REFERENCES

3   *I took the book . . . :* Ronald S. Wallace, *Calvin's Doctrine of the Word and Sacrament* (Edinburgh: Oliver & Boyd, 1953).

4   *She reminded me that . . . one of my favorite professors . . . :* M. G. Kline, *By Oath Consigned: A Reinterpretation of the Covenant Signs of Circumcision and Baptism* (Grand Rapids, MI: Eerdmans, 1968).

5   *He made* covenants *with them . . . :* See O. Palmer Robertson, *The Christ of the Covenants* (Phillipsburg, NJ: Presbyterian and Reformed Publishing Co., 1980).

7   *Such "sacramental realism" . . . :* See Coleman O'Neill, *Sacramental Realism* (Wilmington, DE: Michael Glazier, 1983).

8   *"Protestant worship is at bottom . . .":* Cited in Karl Adam, *The Spirit of Catholicism* (New York: Macmillan, 1933), 187.

9   *"the Catholic sacramental idea":* Ibid., 199.

15 *It was not for His sake that He took flesh . . . :* See C. Vagaggini, *The Flesh: Instrument of Salvation* (Staten Island, NY: Alba House, 1969); E. Schillebeeckx, *Christ the Sacrament of the Encounter with God* (New York: Sheed & Ward, 1963).

18 *They are symbols that genuinely convey . . . :* See L. M. Chauvet, *Symbol and Sacrament: A Sacramental Reinterpre-*

tation of Christian Existence (Collegeville, MN: Liturgical Press, 1995); Karl Rahner, "The Theology of the Symbol," in *Theological Investigations,* vol. 4 (Baltimore: Helicon, 1966), pp. 221–252.

18   *Pope Leo the Great said . . . . :* Sermon 74, quoted in Scott Hahn and Mike Aquilina, *Living the Mysteries: A Guide for Unfinished Christians* (Huntington, IN: Our Sunday Visitor, 2003), p. 261; see also CCC, n. 1075 and 1115.

19   *St. Augustine put it in a memorable way . . . . : Tractates on the Gospel of John,* 6 and 5.18, NPNF Series 1, vol. 7.

19   *Every sacrament produces . . . . :* See B. Leeming, *Principles of Sacramental Theology* (Westminster, MD: Newman Press, 1956), pp. 3–62; P. Pourrat, *Theology of the Sacraments* (St. Louis: B. Herder, 1909), pp. 93–203.

21   *But the priests . . . are not magicians . . . . :* See G. D. Kilpatrick, *The Eucharist in Bible and Liturgy* (New York: Cambridge University Press, 1983), p. 105: "We have then the promises of God. Where this is so, the efficacy of the action performed by man rests on such promises and not on any mechanical process, as is true in magic. By entering into the divine society and by participating in the resultant actions, man commits himself to the covenant proffered by God."

27   *I found them everywhere in the Bible . . . . :* See J. Danielou, *The Bible and the Liturgy* (Notre Dame, IN: University of Notre Dame Press, 1956).

30   *St. Gregory of Nyssa preached a sermon . . . . :* See Hahn and Aquilina, *Living the Mysteries,* p. 44.

30   *St. John of Damascus added . . . . : On the Divine Images* (Crestwood, NY: St. Vladimir's Seminary Press, 2000), p. 23.

31   *Nature itself was a sign . . . :* See Hugh of St. Victor, *On the Sacraments of the Christian Faith* (Cambridge, MA: Medieval Academy of America, 1951), pp. 182–187.

33   *The study of such biblical foreshadowings is called "typology" . . . :* See J. D. Dawson, *Christian Figural Reading and the Fashioning of Identity* (Berkeley: University of California Press, 2002); R. Kuntzmann, *Typologie Biblique* (Paris: Cerf, 2002); F. Ninow, *Indicators of Typology within the Old Testament: The Exodus Motif* (New York: Peter Lang, 2001); C. R. Seitz, *Figured Out: Typology and Providence in Christian Scripture* (Louisville, KY: Westminster John Knox, 2001); Dale C. Allison, *The New Moses: A Matthean Typology* (Minneapolis: Augsburg Fortress, 1993); G. W. Buchanan, *Typology and the Gospel* (New York: University Press of America, 1984); L. Goppelt, Typos: *The Typological Interpretation of the Old Testament in the New* (Grand Rapids, MI: Eerdmans, 1982); R. M. Davidson, *Typology in Scripture: A Study of Hermeneutical* Tupos *Structures* (Berrien Springs, MI: Andrews University Press, 1981); J. Danielou, *From Shadows to Reality: Studies in the Typology of the Fathers* (London: Burns & Oates, 1960); G. W. H. Lampe and K. J. Woollcombe, *Essays on Typology* (London: SCM Press, 1957); F. Foulkes, *The Acts of God: A Study of the Basis of Typology in the Old Testament* (London: Tyndale Press, 1955); A. G. Hebert, *The Throne of David: A Study of the Fulfilment of the Old Testament in Jesus Christ and His Church* (London: Faber & Faber, 1942). For an early attempt to develop a distinctive methodology of "typological criticism," see M. D. Goulder, *Type and History in Acts* (London: SPCK, 1964).

The *Catechism* devotes several paragraphs to typological interpretation in the section on biblical interpretation and elsewhere (CCC 128–130, 1094). On the *Catechism's* teaching on biblical interpretation, see Cardinal J. Ratzinger, *Gospel, Catechesis, Catechism* (San Francisco: Ignatius, 1997), p. 65, n. 24: "It seems to me that there has never been as substantial and comprehensible an introduction to the rudiments of biblical science and interpretation in such a brief format. . . . Given its catechetical function, the *Catechism's* reading of the Bible is essentially spiritual interpretation. Spiritual here does not mean that the exegesis lacks realism or disregards history but that it brings into view the spiritual depth of the historical events." Also see the favorable and balanced treatment of "typology" in the Pontifical Biblical Commission's document, *The Interpretation of the Bible in the Church* (Boston: St. Paul, 1993, pp. 124–125; also see pp. 86–88, 99–101): "The liturgical reform initiated by the Second Vatican Council sought to provide Catholics with rich sustenance from the Bible. The triple cycle of Sunday readings gives a privileged place to the Gospels, in such a way as to shed light on the mystery of Christ as principle of our salvation. By regularly associating a text of the Old Testament with the text of Gospel, the cycle often suggests a scriptural interpretation moving in the direction of typology." On the use of typology in the lectionary and preaching, see Normand Bonneau, *The Sunday Lectionary: Ritual Word, Paschal Shape* (Collegeville, MN: Liturgical Press, 1998); Bonneau, *Preparing the Table of the Word* (Collegeville, MN: Liturgical Press, 1997).

33 *St. Augustine explained: On Christian Doctrine,* I.1–3; II.1–12; III.5–18; Letter 102.33.

34 *These three ages, first sketched out by St. Paul (Rom 5:12–14) . . . :* On the subsequent development of Paul's schematization of salvation history, especially by Augustine *(Propositiones,* 13–18.2; 16.17–23), see P. Fredriksen, "Augustine and Israel," in D. Patte and E. TeSelle (eds.), *Engaging Augustine on Romans* (Harrisburg, PA: Trinity Press International, 2002), pp. 91–110; P. Fredriksen, "Allegory and Reading God's Book: Paul and Augustine on the Destiny of Israel," in J. Whitman (ed.), *Interpretation and Allegory: Antiquity to the Modern Period* (Leiden: E. J. Brill, 2000), pp. 125–149; see especially p. 141: "In Romans, Augustine argued, Paul had organized the history of salvation into a four-stage process: *ante legem* (before the Law), *sub lege* (under the Law), *sub gratia* (under grace), and the final, eschatological stage, *in pace* (in celestial peace). These stages are at once both objective, communal and historical (the experience of humanity from the time before the giving of the Law at Sinai to the second coming of Christ), and also subjective, individual and sequential (the development of the individual toward the moment of conversion—stage 2 to stage 3—and thence ultimately to final redemption in Christ)." This is further elaborated in the twelfth century by Hugh of St. Victor (the "second Augustine"): *On the Sacraments,* pp. 143–204. See R. Moore, *Jews and Christians in the Life and Thought of Hugh of St. Victor* (Atlanta: Scholars Press, 1998), pp. 117–124: "The three divisions of time [nature, law, grace] correspond to three different sacramental remedies, for God's means of restoration varied according

to time" (p. 117). The identical pattern is employed by Bonaventure in his treatment of the sacraments; see *Breviloquium* (Paterson, NJ: St. Anthony Guild Press, 1963), pp. 9, 227–274. For a similar treatment of the "natural" religion of the patriarchal period before Sinai, based on a historical critical approach, see R. W. L. Moberly, *The Old Testament of the Old Testament: Patriarchal Narratives and Mosaic Yahwism* (Minneapolis: Fortress Press, 1992).

34   *St. Thomas Aquinas read the Bible this way: Summa Theologica* I–II, q. 98, 1–5; Thomas Aquinas *Commentary on the Gospel of St. John* (Albany, NY: Magi Books, 1980), pp. 149–153; 433–443. See F. M. Haggard, "An Interpretation of Thomas Aquinas as a Biblical Theologian with Special Reference to His Systematizing of the Economy of Salvation," Ph.D. dissertation, Drew University, 1972.

35   *Thomas explained that each Old Testament type: Commentary on John*, 379.

37   *"For the Holy Spirit is the unfailing fountain . . .": Ibid.,* 435.

40   *Nevertheless, Augustine recognized the special role of the seven sacraments: On Christian Doctrine* 3.9.13; Letter 55.

40-41 *The Council of Florence . . . Council of Trent:* Council of Florence, Session 8; Council of Trent, Session 7, Decree on the Sacraments, canon 1.

42   *"the source and summit of the Christian life":* Vatican II, *Lumen Gentium,* n. 11; see CCC, n. 1324.

42   *"All the other sacraments":* Thomas Aquinas, ST III, 65, 3, see CCC, n. 1211.

43   *"By baptism we are reborn spiritually":* Council of Florence, Session 8.

44   *These three sacraments, according to the Council of Florence: Ibid.*

SOURCES

49   *It is in the Mass that the Scriptures are "actualized" for Christians:* PBC, *Interpretation of the Bible in the Church,* p. 124.

52   *Through ordination, God raises up fathers:* On the paternal authority of the priesthood and the priestly nature of fatherhood, see Richard Sklba, *The Teaching Function of the Pre-Exilic Israelite Priesthood* (Rome: Pontifical University of St. Thomas, 1965), p. 53: "The Patriarchs are described as being active in sacrifice. It seems then that sacrificial and cultic leadership was provided by the head of the family who represented his family in worship. Beside this tradition of patriarchal predominance in the cultic life of the family, we find another tradition which postulates the right of the priesthood in a special way for the first-born son." Also see Fr. Pablo Gadenz, "The Priest as Spiritual Father," in Scott Hahn and Leon Suprenant (eds.), *Catholic for a Reason: Scripture and the Mystery of the Family of God* (Steubenville, OH: Emmaus Road, 1998), pp. 213–234.

59   *Matrimony is ratified by vows and consummated by sexual union:* On the covenantal nature of marriage in Scripture, see Gordon P. Hugenberger, *Marriage as a Covenant* (Leiden: E. J. Brill, 1994). For a profound treatment of the marital sacrament from the perspective of covenant theology, see John S. Grabowski, *Sex and Virtue: An Introduction to Sexual Ethics* (Washington, DC: Catholic University of America Press, 2003), pp. 23–48.

63   *For the ancient Israelites had a word for contract:* See Gene M. Tucker, "Covenant Forms and Contract Forms," *Vetus Testamentum* 15 (1965): 487–503; Paul F. Palmer, "Christian Marriage: Contract or Covenant?" *Theological Studies* 33 (1972): 617–665.

63   *He called it God's* oikonomia . . . : The notion of the "economy" receives great attention and emphasis in the *Catechism of the Catholic Church* (see CCC, nn. 56, 57, 66, 122, 258–260, 705, 1040, 1066, 1076, 1092, 1093, 1095, 1103, 1135, 1159, 1168, 2541, 2606, 2641, 2651, 2666, 2738, 2746, 2758, 2808, 2850). On the meaning and significance of God's "economy" in the writings of the early Church fathers, see R. L. Wilken, *The Spirit of Early Christian Thought* (New Haven, CT: Yale University Press, 2003), pp. 89–92. For a contemporary application, see T. Work, *Living and Active: Scripture in the Economy of Salvation* (Grand Rapids, MI: Eerdmans, 2002).

63   *By covenants, God created and renewed a family bond . . . :* See F. M. Cross, "Kinship and Covenant in Ancient Israel," in *From Epic to Canon: History and Literature in Ancient Israel* (Baltimore: Johns Hopkins University Press, 1998), p. 8: "Oath and covenant, in which the deity is witness, guarantor, or participant, is . . . a widespread legal means by which the duties and privileges of kinship may be extended to another individual or group." Cross adds: "The failure to recognize the rootage of the institution of covenant and covenant obligation in the structures of kinship societies has led to confusion and even gross distortion in the scholarly discussion of the term *berit,* 'covenant,' and in the description of early Israelite religion" (p. 15). Also see G. Quell, *"Diatheke,"* in G. Kittel (ed.), *Theological Dictionary of the New Testament,* vol. 2 (Grand Rapids, MI: Eerdmans, 1964), pp. 114–115: "The legal covenant makes the participants brothers of one bone and one flesh, and thus creates the consequent legal situation. It is a totality . . . which can be no more broken

or altered than the blood relationship itself. . . . There is no firmer guarantee of legal security . . . than the covenant. Regard for the institution is made a religious duty by means of the oath taken at its establishment." Also see Paul Kalluveettil, *Declaration and Covenant: A Comprehensive Review of Covenant Formulae from the Old Testament and the Ancient Near East* (Rome: Pontifical Biblical Institute Press, 1982), pp. 130–135, 203–212; Dennis J. McCarthy, *Treat and Covenant,* 2nd ed. (Rome: Pontifical Biblical Institute Press, 1978), pp. 254–273; F. C. Fensham, "Father and Son as Terminology for Treaty and Covenant," in Hans Goedicke (ed.), *Near Eastern Studies in Honor of William Foxwell Albright* (Baltimore: Johns Hopkins University Press, 1971), pp. 121–135.

63 *The rituals were . . . essential to the relationship:* See CCC, n. 1150; Samson Raphael Hirsch, *The Collected Writings, Volume III: Jewish Symbolism* (New York: Phillipp Feldheim, 1995), pp. 48–50; Bernard J. Cooke, *Christian Sacraments and Christian Personality* (New York: Holt, Rinehart and Winston, 1965), pp. 3–24; G. Martimont, *The Signs of the New Covenant* (Collegeville, MN: Liturgical Press, 1963).

65 *As scholar Walter Bruggemann put it:* W. Bruggemann, "The Covenanted Family," *Journal of Current Social Issues* 14 (1977): 18.

66 *If you were a citizen of ancient Israel—or even Assyria, Greece, or Rome—covenants defined your relationships:* See John Pairman Brown, *Israel and Hellas,* 3 vols. (New York: Walter de Gruyter, 1995–2001), I:253–289; II:135–153; III:152–202; J. T. Fitzgerald, "The Problem of Perjury in Greek Context: Prolegomena to an Exegesis of Matthew

5:33; 1 Timothy 1:10; and *Didache* 2.3," in L. M. White and O. L. Yarbrough (eds.), *The Social World of the First Christians* (Minneapolis: Augsburg Fortress, 1995), pp. 156–177; S. K. Stowers, "Greeks Who Sacrifice and Those Who Do Not: Toward an Anthropology of Greek Religion," in *ibid.*, pp. 293–333; P. Karavites, *Promise-Giving and Treaty-Making: Homer and the Near East* (Leiden: E. J. Brill, 1992), pp. 48–81, 116–200. For similar patterns in Assyria and Babylon, see J. Brinkman, "Political Covenants, Treaties, and Loyalty Oaths in Babylonia and Between Assyria and Babylonia," in L. Canfora (ed.), *I Trattati Nel Mondo Antico Forma Ideologica Funzione* (Rome: Bretschneider, 1990), pp. 81–111; I. M. Price, "The Oath in Court Procedure in Early Babylonia and the Old Testament," *Journal of the American Oriental Society* 49 (1929): 22–29.

67 *To understand the oaths of our ancestors:* See Marvin H. Pope, "Oath," in G. Buttrick (ed.), *The Interpreters Dictionary of the Bible* vol. 3 (New York: Abingdon, 1962), pp. 575–576, who notes how "the oath was an important part of the cult life of the Hebrew community." He adds: "The legal procedure . . . was closely associated with shrines and the priesthood, because the oath as a holy act was properly pronounced in a sacred place or administered by a holy person in contact or connection with holy objects." Also see H. Tadmor, "Treaty and Oath in the Ancient Near East," in G. M. Tucker and D. Knight (eds.), *Humanizing America's Iconic Book* (Chico, CA: Scholars Press, 1982), pp. 127–152; H. S. Gehman, "The Oath in the Old Testament," in J. I. Cook (ed.), *Grace Upon Grace* (Grand Rapids, MI: Eerdmans, 1975),

pp. 51–63; M. R. Lehmann, "Biblical Oaths," *Zeitschrift für die Alttestamentliche Wissenschaft* 81 (1969): 74–91; D. L. Magnetti, "The Oath in the Old Testament in the Light of Related Terms and in the Legal and Covenantal Context of the Ancient Near East," Ph.D. dissertation, Johns Hopkins University, 1969.

For an interesting discussion of oath swearing over a wider range of religions, see Walter Burkert, *Creation of the Sacred* (Cambridge, MA: Harvard University Press, 1996), pp. 163–176. "Why must people have religion? In the ancient world, the obvious answer would have been, for the validation of oaths. Without gods there would be no oaths, and hence no basis for trust and cooperation, for legal action, or for business. . . . Oaths were indispensable in social interactions at all levels, economic and juridical, private and public, intra-tribal and international" (p. 169).

67 *A vow is more weighty:* See T. Cartledge, *Vows in the Hebrew Bible and the Ancient Near East* (Sheffield: JSOT, 1992), pp. 14–16: "Biblical vows and oaths are actually composites of smaller units. The basic building block of both vows and oaths is the *promise:* a person's statement of intention that he or she will or will not do something." Cartledge adds: "Old Testament *oaths* basically consist of a *promise* that is strengthened by the addition of a *curse,* usually . . . with an appeal to the deity . . . who could carry out the curse. While an oath begins with *human* action . . . and moves from there to God's potential response, a vow begins with a plea for *divine* action, followed by a conditional promise of the worshipper's response." Thus, a vow is a conditional human promise made to God, while an oath consists of a promise rein-

forced by the invocation of God's name for judgment (blessing or curse).

68 *This manner of judgment is built into the ancient understanding of oaths:* See J. S. Anderson, "The Social Function of Curses in the Hebrew Bible," *Zeitschrift fur die Alttestamentliche Wissenschaft* 110 (1998): 223–237; J. J. Pilch, "The Power of the Curse," *The Bible Today* (September 1998): 313–317; T. G. Crawford, *Blessing and Curse in Syro-Palestinian Inscriptions* (New York: Peter Lang, 1992); J. Plescia, *The Oath and Perjury in Ancient Greece* (Tallahassee: Florida State University Press, 1970); H. C. Brichto, *The Problem of "Curse" in the Hebrew Bible* (Philadelphia: Society of Biblical Literature, 1963); S. H. Blank, "The Curse, Blasphemy, the Spell, and the Oath," *Hebrew Union College Annual* 23 (1950–51): 73–95.

69 *When offered in the context of a covenant oath, a sacrifice:* See Dennis J. McCarthy, "Further Notes on the Symbolism of Blood and Sacrifice," *Journal of Biblical Literature* 92 (1973): 207; he describes a covenant "oath sacrifice" as "a conditional self-curse in which the curse is reinforced by a symbolic action." See McCarthy, "Covenant and Law in Chronicles-Nehemiah," *Catholic Biblical Quarterly* 44 (1982): 37: "Finally, it is an oath which guarantees renewal of the covenant . . . [where] the sacrifices associated with covenant-renewal are the basic element." Also see Z. P. Thundyil, *Covenant in Anglo-Saxon Thought* (Calcutta: Macmillan Company of India, 1972), pp. 198–199, who explains how "the oath was . . . an act of cult or worship. . . . Oaths were often accompanied by sacrifices and holocausts which were covenant rituals." On oath sacrifice in ancient Greece, see W. Burkert,

Greek Religion (Cambridge, MA: Harvard University Press, 1985), pp. 250–304; Burkert, Homo Necans: *The Anthropology of Ancient Greek Sacrificial Ritual and Myth* (Berkeley: University of California Press, 1983), pp. 29–82. Plescia, *Oath and Perjury,* pp. 9–10: "Generally speaking, there was no important oath without a sacrifice and a libation" (Plescia then cites several examples).

70   *"It is generally believed . . .":* Nahum Sarna, *Understanding Genesis: The Heritage of Biblical Israel* (New York: Schocken, 1966), p. 126.

71   *Some scholars have proposed that the word* berith *derives from . . . "meal":* See W. Weinfeld, *"Berith,"* in G. Botterweck and H. Ringgren (eds.), *Theological Dictionary of the Old Testament,* vol. 2 (Grand Rapids, MI: Eerdmans, 1975), p. 253: *"berith* is a fem. Noun from *brh,* 'to eat, dine' . . . and refers to the festive meal accompanying the covenantal ceremony."

72   *many rabbis have interpreted:* Baruch Levine, *Leviticus* (Philadelphia: Jewish Publication Society, 1989), pp. xxxviii, 11. See also Levine, *In the Presence of the Lord* (Leiden: E. J. Brill, 1974), p. 38.

73   *the earliest Christians spoke of the Mass:* See *Didache* 14, where the word appears three times in a short passage regarding the liturgy.

77   Ex opere operato: *what a strange and wonderful phrase:* See Plescia, *Oath and Perjury in Ancient Greece,* p. 49, n. 55: "The formula of the oath acted *ex opere operato,* that is, by the automatic efficacy of the ritual words of the formula." Also see J. G. Griffiths, *The Divine Verdict: A Study of Divine Judgement in the Ancient Religions* (Leiden: E. J. Brill, 1991).

79   *Pliny the Younger:* From *Letters,* X.96–97: "An anonymous
pamphlet was issued, containing a number of names of al-
leged Christians. Those who denied that they were or
had been Christians and called upon the gods with the
usual formula, reciting the words after me, and those who
offered incense and wine before your image—which I
had ordered to be brought forward for this purpose, along
with the regular statues of the gods—all such I considered
acquitted—especially as they cursed the name of Christ,
which it is said *bona fide* Christians cannot be induced to
do. Still others there were, whose names were supplied by
an informer. These first said they were Christians, then
denied it, insisting they had been, 'but were so no longer';
some of them having 'recanted many years ago,' and more
than one 'full twenty years back.' These all worshiped
your image and the gods' statues and cursed the name of
Christ. But they declared their guilt or error was simply
this—on a fixed day they used to meet before dawn and
recite a hymn among themselves to Christ, as though he
were a god. So far from binding themselves by oath to
commit any crime, they swore to keep from theft, rob-
bery, adultery, breach of faith, and not to deny any trust
money deposited with them when called upon to deliver
it. This ceremony over, they used to depart and meet
again to take food, but it was of no special character, and
entirely harmless." For an online version of this text, see:
http://ccat.sas.upenn.edu/jod/texts/pliny.html.

80   *"This swearing of the* sacramentum . . .*":* See "The Recruit
of the Republican Army," taken from a chapter in the online version of "The Illustrated History of the Roman
Empire," www.roman-empire.net/army/becoming.html.

81   *The* sacramentum *was, in the gentile world:* See E. O. James, *Sacrifice and Sacrament* (New York: Barnes and Noble, 1962), p. 232: "In Roman law . . . the word *sacramentum* was used to describe a legal religious sanction in which a man placed his life or property in the hands of the supernatural powers who upheld justice and honoured solemn engagements and contracts. It then became an oath of allegiance . . . (taken by soldiers to their *imperator*), sworn under a formula having a religious connotation. In the Early Church it was given a numinous and esoteric interpretation when the Latin *sacer* was brought into conjunction with the Greek *mysterion*. Thus, it became a convenient term for efficacious sacred signs or symbols which convey something 'hidden'—a mysterious potency transmitted through material instruments as appointed channels of divine grace in a ritual observance." See Kline, *By Oath Consigned,* p. 81: "As an oath-sign of allegiance to Christ the Lord, baptism is a sacrament in the original sense of *sacramentum* in its etymological relation to the idea of consecration, and more particularly in its employment for the military oath of allegiance." George E. Mendenhall and Gary A. Herion, "Covenant," in David N. Freedman (ed.), *The Anchor Bible Dictionary,* vol. 2 (New York: Doubleday, 1992), p. 1198: "Latin *sacramentum* at the time of the early Church referred to a soldier's oath of loyalty to the Roman emperor." "This brings us back to the late developments in ANE thought when covenants had come to be regarded primarily as 'loyalty oaths.' No doubt this formal similarity between concepts of 'covenant' facilitated the communication of early Christianity in the non-Palestinian environment of

Mediterranean civilization." Also see M. Weinfeld, "The
Loyalty Oath in the Ancient Near East," *Ugarit-Forschun-
gen* 8 (1976): 385: "Most surprising is the similarity between the clauses of a loyalty oath from the Roman
period in which the vassals pledge to revere the Caesar
more than themselves and their sons, and the similar
clauses in the Hittite documents." He adds: "It is difficult
to contend that such a full overlapping with the Near
Eastern loyalty oaths is purely coincidental, and it is our
opinion that the oath of loyalty to the Roman Emperor
has its roots in an ancient Near Eastern tradition." He
shows parallels with the Athenian league (p. 385) and the
mystery sects (p. 406): "The new initiate's oath was considered a *sacramentum* and was like a soldier's oath of loyalty . . . the members of the mystery sect being called
militia." Similar practices and patterns are evident among
ancient Jews (p. 406): "This phenomenon elucidates well
Philo's conception of Israel's entry into the covenant. The
entrance into the covenant in Dt. 29:11–14 is understood
by Philo to be like an initiation into a mystery-sect *(mys-
tagogon)*." Weinfeld also cites a speech by the fourth-
century Greek orator Andocides ("On the Mysteries"),
who declares that "all the Athenians shall take oath . . .
over a sacrifice without blemish" (p. 389). For more on
the religious background of oath-swearing ritual in ancient Greece, see Walter Burkert, *Savage Energies: Lessons
of Myth and Ritual in Ancient Greece* (Chicago: University
of Chicago Press, 2001); W. Burkert, *The Orientalizing
Revolution: Near Eastern Influence on Greek Culture in the
Early Archaic Period* (Cambridge, MA: Harvard University
Press, 1992); J. D. Mikalson, *Religion in Hellenistic Athens*

(Berkeley: University of California Press, 1998); J. D. Mikalson, *Honor They Gods: Popular Religion in Greek Tragedy* (Chapel Hill: University of North Carolina Press, 1991); J. D. Mikalson, *Athenian Popular Religion* (Chapel Hill: University of North Carolina Press, 1983), pp. 83–105; M. Detienne and Jean-Pierre Vernant, *Cuisine of Sacrifice Among the Greeks* (Chicago: University of Chicago Press, 1989).

81   *His name was Tertullian:* On Tertullian's covenantal under-standing and use of *sacramentum,* see D. Michaelides, *Sacramentum Chez Tertullien* (Paris: Etudes Augustini-ennes, 1970). Also see C. P. Price, "Mysteries and Sacra-ments," in A. J. Hultgen and B. Hall (eds.), *Christ and His Communities* (Cincinnati: Forward Movement Publica-tions, 1990), pp. 124–139; A. D. Nock, "Hellenistic Mys-teries and Christian Sacraments," in Z. Steward (ed.), *Essays on Religion and the Ancient World,* vol. 2 (Cam-bridge, MA: Harvard University Press, 1972), pp. 791–820.

83   *And the ancient rabbis ruled that every blessing must meet with the response:* Eric Werner, *The Sacred Bridge: Liturgical Par-allels in Synagogue and Early Church* (New York: Schocken Books, 1970), p. 209.

84   *When the Romans persecuted Christians:* Robert M. Grant, "Sacrifices and Oaths as Required of Early Christians," in P. Granfield and J. A. Jungmann (eds.), *Kyriakon: Festschrift Johannes Quasten,* vol. 1 (Munster: Verlag As-chendorff, 1970), pp. 12–17.

85   *"When you renounce Satan . . ."*: Cyril, *Catechetical Lecture* 19.9; see E. Yarnold, *The Awe-Inspiring Rites of Initiation* (Collegeville, MN: Liturgical Press, 1994), p. 74.

85   *Today we call it "exorcism":* See David E. Aune, "Exorcism," in G. W. Bromiley (ed.), *International Standard Bible Encyclopedia,* vol. 2, rev. ed. (Grand Rapids, MI: Eerdmans, 1982), p. 242: "A word derived from the Gk. *Exorkizein,* meaning 'adjure,' 'charge (someone) under oath'. . . . Exorcism may be defined as the process of expelling an evil spirit or spirits from a possessed individual through the means of adjurations and rituals. Oaths are important in exorcism, and . . . almost always a central feature of exorcistic formulas."

90   *"an ancient ruin still standing" "Oaths are fossils of piety":* George E. Mendenhall, *Law and Covenant in Israel and the Ancient Near East* (Pittsburgh: Biblical Colloquium, 1955), p. 26; George Santayana, quoted in Geoffrey Hughes, *Swearing: A Social History of Foul Language, Oaths, and Profanity in English* (Oxford: Blackwell, 1991), p. 1. Cf. V. Eller, *The Promise* (Garden City, NY: Doubleday, 1970), pp. 184–185: "What sort of theology lies behind the use of oath? Medieval superstition, that's what!" "Oath-swearing represents man's baldest sort of attempt to make God into a bottled genie used to serve his own petty purposes."

90   *Joseph Vining, a renowned legal scholar:* J. Vining, *The Authoritative and the Authoritarian* (Chicago: University of Chicago Press, 1986), p. 188. He makes some provocative observations: "Where else do free, grown, thinking and sane men and women behave in this way and in such an atmosphere? Where else do individuals in robes sit on a raised dais in the center of a room designed to evoke awe and respect? Where else do men conceive of themselves as supplicating, and say explicitly that they are praying for

relief? Where else can be found men and women dressed in their best and most sober clothes engaging in self-abasement, where respect enforced by custom and discipline, where absence of direct challenge, use of titles, faith demanded at the outset? Where else but the church?" (p. 190). He continues the comparison with theologians and lawyers: "They all look to authoritative texts. This they do not just for the regulation of their ritual behavior, for which the authority of the text is almost a matter of definition. At least in the Western world questions about what to do in the world and how to think are settled by appeals to authority. If the authoritative statement is uttered by an official, it is made after reference to an argument about written texts. The agreement of religions on this point, this point of method, and their identity in this regard with law, is remarkable" (p. 190). Also see G. W. Buchanan, *Biblical and Theological Insights from Ancient and Modern Civil Law* (Lewiston, NY: Edwin Mellen Press, 1992); R. K. Fenn, *Liturgies and Trials* (Oxford: Basil Blackwell, 1982).

93   *Lyndon B. Johnson . . . described that reality:* M. A. Pauley, *I Do Solemnly Swear: The President's Constitutional Oath* (New York: University Press of America, 1999), p. 5.

93   *"swearing puts on record my spiritual assumption . . .":* J. L. Austin, *How to Do Things with Words* (New York: Oxford University Press, 1962), p. 10. On speech-act theory, see T. Ward, *Word and Supplement: Speech Acts, Biblical Texts and the Sufficiency of Scripture* (New York: Oxford University Press, 2002); R. S. Briggs, *Words in Action: Speech Act Theory and Biblical Interpretation* (Edinburgh: T. & T. Clark, 2001); K. J. Vanhoozer, "From Speech Acts to

Scripture Acts: The Covenant of Discourse and the Discourse of Covenant," in C. Bartholomew et al. (eds.), *After Pentecost: Language and Biblical Interpretation* (Grand Rapids, MI: Zondervan, 2001), pp. 1–49; D. Patrick, *The Rhetoric of Revelation in the Hebrew Bible* (Minneapolis, MN: Augsburg Fortress, 1999); A Donghi, *Actions and Words: Symbolic Language and the Liturgy* (Collegeville, MN: Liturgical Press, 1997); N. Wolterstorff, *Divine Discourse: Philosophical Reflections on the Claim that God Speaks* (New York: Cambridge University Press, 1995); A. C. Thiselton, *Interpreting God and the Postmodern Self: On Meaning, Manipulation and Promise* (Edinburgh: T. & T. Clark: Eerdmans, 1995); A. Viberg, *Symbols of Law: A Contextual Analysis of Legal Symbolic Acts in the Old Testament* (Stockholm: Almqvist & Wiksell, 1992); D. Evans, *The Logic of Self-Involvement* (New York: Herder and Herder, 1969).

95   *"There can be no religious society . . ."*: Augustine, *Reply to Faustus the Manichaean* 19.11, www.newadvent.org/fathers/140619.htm.

95   *"How can something which is bread . . ."*: On the Sacraments 4.14–16; in Yarnold, *Awe-Inspiring Rites of Initiation,* pp. 132–133.

96   *"Everything could well have been done . . ."*: Augustine, *On Christian Doctrine,* prologue 6, quoted in Peter Brown, *Augustine of Hippo* (Berkeley: University of California Press, 1967), pp. 267–268.

96   *"The bread is at first common bread . . ."*: St. Gregory of Nyssa, *On the Baptism of Christ,* www.newadvent.org/fathers/2910.htm.

97   *"Take away the word . . .":* Augustine, *Tractates on the Gospel of John* 80.3, www.newadvent.org/fathers/1701080.htm.

101   *"The physically perceptible world . . .":* Samson Raphael Hirsch, *The Collected Writings, Volume III: Jewish Symbolism* (New York: Phillipp Feldheim, 1995), p. 101. See K. J. Dell, "Covenant and Creation in Relationship," in A. D. H. Mayes and R. B. Salters (eds.), *Covenant as Context* (New York: Oxford University Press, 2003), pp. 111–133; Robert Murray, *The Cosmic Covenant: Biblical Themes of Justice, Peace and the Integrity of Creation* (London: Sheed & Ward, 1992), pp. 1–13; Roland de Vaux, *Ancient Israel: Its Life and Institutions* vol. 2 (New York: McGraw-Hill, 1961), p. 481: "Creation is the first action in the history of salvation; once it was over, God stopped work, and he was then able to make a covenant. . . . The 'sign' of the Covenant made at the dawn of creation is the observance of the sabbath . . ."

103   *"And this oath is mighty . . .":* 1 Enoch 69.15–27; see J. H. Charlesworth (ed.), *The Old Testament Pseudepigrapha: Apocalyptic Literature and Testaments* (New York: Doubleday, 1983), pp. 47–49; Murray, *Cosmic Covenant,* pp. 7–13; M. Barker, *The Great High Priest: The Temple Roots of Christian Liturgy* (New York: T. & T. Clark, 2003), pp. 197–201; M. Barker, *The Lost Prophet: The Book of Enoch and Its Influence on Christianity* (Nashville, TN: Abingdon, 1988); M. Barker, "The Book of Enoch and Cosmic Sin," *The Ecologist* (January/February 2000): 30ff. This is echoed in *Sifre Deuteronomy* 330: "When the Holy One, blessed be He, created, He did not create . . . except by an oath . . ."

103   *Ever afterward, it was in imitation of God that men swore covenant oaths by sevening themselves:* See *The Hebrew & Aramaic Lexicon of the Old Testament: The New Koehler-Baumgartner in English,* vol. 4 (Leiden: E. J. Brill, 1999), p. 1396: "The radical consonants of the verb suggest some connection with the common Semitic numeral *sheva'* seven, and also with II *sheva',* cf. Arb. *sabaga* 'to be ample, be complete.'" See Moshe Greenberg, "Oath," in Cecil Roth (ed.), *Encyclopedia Judaica,* vol. 12 (Jerusalem: Keter, 1971), p. 1296: "The close link between oath and curse lends color to the suggested derivation of the terms *hishbi'a',* 'adjure,' *nishba',* 'swear,' and *shevu'ah,* 'oath,' from *sheva',* 'seven,' based on the use of seven in maledictions. . . . The original sense might have been 'to lay [curses in] sevens on someone' or 'to take [curses in] sevens on oneself.' Sevens are also associated with oaths . . . in Gen. 21:27–31 and Num. 23." See M. R. Lehmann, "Biblical Oaths," *Zeitschrift fur die Alttestamentliche Wissenschaft* 81 (1969): 79: "We may now conclude . . . the number 7 is indeed an essential feature in oath-ceremonies, in Biblical as well as extra-biblical sources." Lehmann adds: "In the case of oaths, we propose that the *basic* meaning of the oath was: seven animals killed in the presence of the parties to the oath, with the explicit or implicit meaning 'may the fate of these seven befall the one who breaks the oath!' It is now obvious why in Hebrew the verb 'to swear' . . . is in the Nif'al, the passive—since it undoubtedly stands for 'to be made subject to the (fate of the) seven' or 'to take upon oneself the (fate of the) seven.'" Also see F. Brown, S. R. Driver, C. A. Briggs (eds.), *A Hebrew and English Lexicon of the Old Tes-*

tament (London: Oxford University Press, 1907), pp. 989–990. Also see the meditations of the father of modern Orthodox Judaism, Rabbi Hirsch, *Jewish Symbolism,* p. 99: "In each of the above Biblical passages the number seven is used to express a full number . . . something 'whole' or 'complete.' "

105 *"You shall not take the name of the Lord your God in vain . . .":* See Lehmann, "Biblical Oaths," p. 80: "The usual translation is 'You must not invoke the name of the Lord your God in evil intent (or: in vain).' This translation infers that the prohibition is directed against every profane or unnecessary use of the divine name. . . . Since we have observed the role of God as the executioner of the curses inherent in an oath, the Biblical prohibition is actually a warning that God will not free . . . the one swearing falsely from the consequences of the curse which he takes upon himself. The correct translation should be 'You must not swear in God's name falsely for the Lord will not free (from curses) him who swears falsely in his name, and breaks against the oath he has taken upon himself.' "

106 *To break this covenant was to release forces which could destroy Creation:* See M. Barker, "The Book of Enoch and Cosmic Sin," pp. 30ff.; Murray, *Cosmic Covenant,* pp. 14–26.

106 *Perjury committed by one:* Hirsch, *Jewish Symbolism,* pp. 101–102.

109 *Jesus bore all the curses of the previously broken covenants:* See James Swetnam, "A Suggested Interpretation of Hebrews 9:15–18," *Catholic Biblical Quarterly* 27 (1965): 381: "Christ, by taking on himself the curse stipulations which in the first *diatheke* were connected with transgressions,

was able to draw up and effect a *diatheke* which makes efficacious provision only for blessings." Also see F. C. Fensham, "The Curse of the Cross and the Renewal of the Covenant," in *Biblical Essays* (Stellenbosch: University of Stellenbosch, 1966), pp. 219–226.

111   *One of the native tribes, the Gibeonites:* See R. P. Gordon, "Gibeonite Ruse and Israelite Curse in Joshua 9," in A. D. H. Mayes and R. B. Salters (eds.), *Covenant as Context* (New York: Oxford University Press, 2003): 163–190; F. C. Fensham, "The Treaty Between Israel and the Gibeonites," *Biblical Archaeologist* 27 (1964): 96–100.

111   *King Saul, perhaps, did not consider oaths as truly binding:* For an excellent treatment of "Oaths in Biblical Narrative," see Hugh S. Pyper, *David as Reader: 2 Samuel 12:1–15 and the Poetics of Fatherhood* (Leiden: E. J. Brill, 1996), pp. 131–155. Pyper observes: "There has been remarkably little discussion of the oath forms of the Old Testament and what there has been concentrates, not unexpectedly, on philology and comparative linguistics rather than on the narratological functions of the oath" (p. 131). Besides the many biblical examples that Pyper considers, there are as many as seven oaths in the two-chapter narrative drama of Solomon's royal accession (1 Kgs 1:13; 1:17–18; 1:29–31; 1:51; 2:8–9; 2:23–25; 2:42–43). Also see D. Friedmann, *To Kill and Take Possession: Law, Morality and Society in Biblical Stories* (Peabody, MA: Hendrickson, 2002), pp. 9–61, 145–164.

115   *"the number seven [is] also meant . . .":* Hirsch, *Jewish Symbolism,* p. 103.

118   *"In every city of Greece . . .":* Xenophon, *Memorabilia* 4.4.16, cited by Plescia, *Oath and Perjury in Ancient*

Greece, p. 18. Plescia shows how legitimacy was established in Athens by a paternal oath, but when Athenian youth reached their eighteenth year, "he took the so-called ephebic oath publicly in the temple" (p. 16). This entailed two years of compulsory military service, but "through this oath, the young man . . . became part of the polis" (p. 17). He notes: "If an ordinary citizen, in order to enjoy the rights of citizenship, had to submit to an oath, then a fortiori the citizen who was to take a government position. . . . In fact, the confidence inspired by an oath encouraged the Greeks, and for that matter all nations, to impose upon those who were in authority or were invested with a public function the bonds of an oath, in order to make them fulfill their public duties loyally" (p. 24; also see Aristotle's Commentary on the Athenian Constitution, 55). Plescia observes how citizens were thus enrolled in the *leitourgia,* as civil servants of the common good, that is, "public duty at one's own expense" (p. 32).

118   *"All the Athenians shall take this oath . . .": Ibid.,* p. 21.

119   *"Peace is secured by the oaths . . .":* Letter 47.2 in Augustine, *Letters* vol. 1 (Washington, DC: Catholic University of America Press, 1951), p. 227.

119   *"The law and civil polity of England . . .":* Cited in D. M. Jones, *Conscience and Allegiance in Seventeenth Century England: The Political Significance of Oaths* (New York: University of Rochester Press, 1999), p. 61. Similar convictions are later expressed by John Locke: "Those who deny the existence of the Deity are not to be tolerated at all. Promises, covenants and oaths, which are the bonds of human society, can have no hold upon or sanctity for an

225

atheist. For the taking away of God, even only in thought, dissolves all" (*A Letter on Toleration* [Oxford: Oxford University Press, 1968], p. 135).

119   *"Let it simply be asked . . .":* Pauley, *I Do Solemnly Swear,* p. 113; see The Avalon Project at Yale Law School, www.yale.edu/lawweb/avalon/washing.htm.

120   *Until very recently, all medical doctors had to swear the Hippocratic Oath:* See Patrick G. D. Riley, "Medicine as Moral Art: The Hippocratic Philosophy of Herbert Ratner, M.D.," *Linacre Quarterly* 65 (November 1998): 5–38. "Medicine became a profession . . . precisely because its members professed an oath. Moreover medicine was the first calling to require an oath of its members, and hence was the first profession. The other professions that followed—the learned professions of law and divinity, and the military—all became professions because they too took oaths" (p. 20). See P. Carrick, *Medical Ethics in the Ancient World* (Washington, DC: Georgetown University Press, 2001), pp. 83–112; N. Cameron, *The New Medicine: Life and Death After Hippocrates* (Wheaton, IL: Crossway Books, 1991); Ludwig Edelstein, *The Hippocratic Oath* (Baltimore: Johns Hopkins Press, 1943); W. H. S. Jones, *The Doctor's Oath* (Cambridge: Cambridge University Press, 1924).

120   *"Power tends to corrupt . . .":* Lord Acton, Letter to Bishop Mandell Creighton, 1887, in Gertrude Himmelfarb (ed.), *Essays on Freedom and Power* (Cleveland, OH: Meridian Books, 1972), pp. 335–336.

122   *when George Washington took the oath of office:* See Pauley, *I Do Solemnly Swear,* p. 109.

128   *God's name makes all the difference:* See Ephraim E. Urbach,

"The Power of the Divine Name," *The Sages: Their Concepts and Beliefs* (Jerusalem: Magnes, 1979), pp. 124–134; Chaim Kaplan, "The Hidden Name," *Journal of the Society of Oriental Research* 13 (1927): 181–184.

132   *"It seems to me that this was said . . .":* Augustine, *Letter to Publicola,* 47.2; for an online version: www.newadvent.org/fathers/1102047.htm.

132   *Jesus Himself used oaths in His speech:* See J. P. Brown, *Israel and Hellas,* vol. 3, p. 216: "Jesus needed to certify sayings by a formula, which as it seems inherited the oath-grammar. Rabbinic has the same grammar for an oath as Biblical Hebrew. The woman suspected of adultery (Num 5,20) takes an oath with 'Amen' . . ."

135   *Job's oath . . . is a reverent oath:* See J. E. Hartley, "From Lament to Oath: A Study of Progression in the Speeches of Job," in W. A. M. Beuken (ed.), *The Book of Job* (Leuven: University Press, 1994), pp. 79–100; Meredith G. Kline, "Trial by Ordeal," in W. Godfrey and J. Boyd (eds.), *Through Christ's Word* (Phillipsburg, NJ: Presbyterian and Reformed, 1985), pp. 81–93.

138   *"When a man takes an oath . . .":* Robert Bolt, *A Man for All Seasons* (New York: Vintage, 1962), p. 81.

141   *"abiding in God, being made like God . . .":* St. Basil the Great, *On the Holy Spirit* 9.23, www.newadvent.org/fathers/3201000.htm.

142   *The famous modern biblical scholar:* George E. Mendenhall, *Ancient Israel's Faith and History* (Louisville, KY: Westminster John Knox Press, 2001), pp. 227–229. See K. van der Toorn, *Sin and Sanction in Israel and Mesopotamia* (Assen: Van Gorcum, 1985), pp. 40–55. Van der Toorn observes how covenant oaths in ancient Israel and Mesopotamia

are often "couched as prayers," which took various forms, such as the "oath by water and oil," or the more dangerous *asakku*, where "the oath taker was given some sacred substance to eat, which would prove fatal in case of perjury" (p. 46).

149   *"Let all mortal flesh keep silence . . .":* "Let All Mortal Flesh Keep Silence," adapted from the Liturgy of St. James; translated from the Greek by Gerard Moultrie, 1864.

150   *martyrs of Abitina:* Andre Hamman, *The Mass: Ancient Liturgies and Patristic Texts* (Staten Island, NY: Alba House, 1967), p. 16. See Robin Darling Young, *In Procession Before the World: Martyrdom as Public Liturgy in Early Christianity* (Milwaukee: Marquette University Press, 2001).

154   *"The renewal in the Eucharist . . .":* Sacrosanctum Concilium: Consititution on the Sacred Liturgy 10; for an online version: www.vatican.va

157   *Indeed, the act that consummates the covenant is sexual intercourse:* See Hugenberger, *Marriage as a Covenant,* pp. 240–278. On marriage as a covenantal metaphor, see R. Abma, *Bonds of Love: Methodic Studies of Prophetic Texts with Marriage Imagery* (Assen: Van Gorcum, 1999); N. Stienstra, *YHWH Is the Husband of His People* (Kampen: Kok Pharos, 1993).

157   *The law stated in Deuteronomy:* See Hugenberger, *Marriage as a Covenant,* pp. 249–250.

177   *When Muslim theologians dispute the plausibility . . .:* This viewpoint is expressed by Bernard G. Weiss, a professor of Islamic studies, in "Covenant and Law in Islam," in E. B. Firmage et al. (eds.), *Religion and Law: Biblical-Judaic and Islamic Perspectives* (Winona Lake, IN: Eisenbrauns, 1990), pp. 72–73: "Swearing is, in fact, a kind of

covenanting. However, the divine covenant cannot be described as a swearing, for God by definition cannot swear to anything. Swearing is an acting of binding one's self to something. . . . But God cannot . . . be bound or limited by anything, and by the same token he cannot swear to anything."

178 *The very reason for the incarnation was so that God could bear the covenant curse . . .:* See D. McCartney and C. Clayton, *Let the Reader Understand: A Guide to Interpreting and Applying the Bible* (Wheaton, IL: Victor Books, 1994), p. 190: "But in this case God took the oath, invoking the curse on Himself as guarantee of the fulfillment of His promises. So justification by faith was possible because of God's sworn promises. . . . And when Abraham's descendants rebelled against the covenant, the curse of death devolved upon God Himself incarnate."

178 *The earliest sacramental manual . . .:* J. B. Lightfoot and J. R. Harmer, *The Apostolic Fathers* (Grand Rapids, MI: Baker, 1984), p. 235. Also see N. Pardee, "The Curse that Saves *(Didache* 16.5)," in N. Jefford (ed.), *The Didache in Context* (Leiden: E. J. Brill, 1995), pp. 156–176.

183 *They called it* parousia *. . . :* See A. Souter, *A Pocket Lexicon to the Greek New Testament* (Oxford: Clarendon Press, 1966), p. 194. Several biblical texts use *parousia* in the sense of "(mere) presence" (2 Cor 10:10; Phil 2:12). See the comments on the use of the term in 1 Thessalonians 4:15 in G. K. Beale, *1–2 Thessalonians* (Downers Grove, IL: InterVarsity Press, 2003), pp. 139–140: "What has been traditionally understood as the second coming of Christ is best conceived as a revelation of his formerly hidden, heavenly 'presence.' The references to *parousia* in

2:19, 3:13 and 5:23 also carry the same connotation. When Christ appears, he will not descend from the sky over Boston or London or New York City or Hong Kong or any other localized area. When he appears, the present dimension will be ripped away, and Christ will be manifest to all eyes throughout the earth (see Mt 24:27). . . . How this is possible in literal geographical terms is certainly unclear, but the answer lies in recalling that a new dimension will break into the old physical dimension, and the possibilities of new kinds of perception and of existence beyond present understanding will then be realized. Interestingly, Revelation 21:3, 22 say that directly following Christ's final coming, God and the Lamb will form a 'tabernacling' presence over all redeemed believers. . . . The figurative nature of the language is also pointed to by reference to the trumpet call of God (1 Thes 4:16), which is like the blowing of the trumpets in Revelation or like God's throne in heaven or Christ as a heavenly lamb . . ." Beale further notes: "If John were living today, he might use the analogy of a stage curtain with pictures on it, which is drawn from both sides to reveal the actors behind it. In short, the present physical reality will in some way disappear and the formerly hidden heavenly dimension, where Christ and God dwell, will be revealed (see further Rev 11:19; 19:11; 21:1–3)," p. 138.

184 *The great historical theologian Jaroslav Pelikan, writing as a Lutheran . . .:* J. Pelikan, *The Christian Tradition: A History of the Development of Doctrine, Vol. I: The Emergence of the Catholic Tradition (100–600)* (Chicago: University of Chicago Press, 1971), p. 126. See O. Cullmann, *Essays on the Lord's Supper* (London: Lutterworth, 1958), p. 15:

"Hence, in the early Church, the Lord's Supper involved the presence of Christ in its threefold relation with Easter, with the cult and with the *Parousia.*" See M. Barker, "*Parousia* and Liturgy," in *The Revelation of Jesus Christ* (Edinburg: T. & T. Clark, 2000), pp. 373–388; E. Mazza, *Mystagogy: A Theology of Liturgy in the Patristic Age* (New York: Pueblo, 1989), pp. 167–169; S. Hahn, "Come Again? The Real Presence as *Parousia,*" in *Scripture Matters: Essays on Reading the Bible from the Heart of the Church*" (Steubenville, OH: Emmaus Road, 2003), pp. 119–135.

185   *A good friend of mine refers to this as "the real presence of the marital bond."* See Leon Suprenant, "The 'Real Presence' of the Marital Bond," in S. Hahn and L. Suprenant (eds.), *Catholic for a Reason: Scripture and the Mystery of the Family of God* (Steubenville, OH: Emmaus Road, 1999), pp. 237–264.

186   *Kimberly is not only my vocation . . .* See my wife's (much deeper) insights in K. Hahn, *Life-Giving Love: Embracing God's Beautiful Design for Marriage* (Ann Arbor, MI: Servant, 2002).

186   *Since marriage is a sacrament, family life is a kind of domestic liturgy . . .:* See CCC nn. 1623, 1631, 1657.

188   *He wants all the world to be taken up into His liturgy . . .:* See S. Hahn, *The Lamb's Supper: The Mass as Heaven on Earth* (New York: Doubleday, 1999). Also see CCC n. 1329: "The Lord's Supper . . . anticipates the wedding feast of the Lamb in the heavenly Jerusalem."

199   *We should read that chapter often and savor it:* See J. Dunnill, *Covenant and Sacrifice in the Letter to the Hebrews* (New York: Cambridge University Press, 1992), p. 249: "Oaths

and the finality they confer are deeply important in Hebrews, especially the unique status and revolutionary consequences of *divine* oaths." Also see S. Hahn, "Kinship by Covenant: A Biblical-Theological Analysis of Covenant Types and Texts in the Old and New Testaments" (Ph.D. dissertation, Marquette University, 1995), pp. 57–75, 549–565. "There are no convincing parallels in the pagan world, whether in the more typical case of God as suzerain binding Israel to serve Him or in the more unusual position of God binding Himself by oath to the service of his own servants" (D. N. Freedman, "Divine Commitment and Human Obligation," *Int* 18 [1964]: p. 420).